THE SCHIZOPHRENIA DIARIES

*For Mom, who held my hand all through my past.
For Kate, who showed me a hopeful future.*

*(And for all the artists and beyond who took
me in when sane society threw me out.)*

CONTENTS

MY SCHIZOPHRENIA TAMAGOTCHI

"Farrah's back," I said at brunch. "She seems to like mornings."

It was a morning just days ago, near the one year anniversary of my father's death, when Farrah appeared for the first time. A puppy hiding between the edge of a desk and the wall. She never got too close, but when I paid particular attention to her, I could, unbidden, feel her warm fur in my fingers. The tactile hallucinations were relatively new, too. I wasn't complaining about this one in particular, though; it was much less terrifying and consuming than the others as recent as last night, almost soothing except for the nature of hallucinating and knowing it.

The name Farrah was printed on the silver dog bone shaped tag on her red leather collar, the kind of bright red that made more sense for the ribbon you put on the puppy on Christmas morning than the stiff material the hue appeared on. The color appeared almost scribbled over the texture rather than a part of it. I could read the name only when it came as a zoomed in flash of an image,

"

and I think I *felt* it more than read it. I didn't know why Farrah. Google later revealed an Arabic origin, a girl's name meaning joy.

Rather benign for a manifestation of mental illness.

After first noting Farrah's appearance, I noted that sometimes when I changed rooms—she was highly reactive to the real environment, a trend for my hallucinations lately, pawing at the unknowing actual cats curiously, hiding in real nooks—she vanished from the real environment, but came to me in flashes of moments when I started to dissociate. Trying to describe where she was in those flashes, I told my fiancee that it was like a computer game I'd played as a kid—there was a dog in an unexciting space without much to do but pet its head and throw a ball and give it a treat and have it look cute and do tricks. Having not played the game I had in mind, she, more of a nineties kid than me, came up with something similar enough:

"Oh, like a tamagotchi."

This set me off in a long giggling fit I couldn't stop. "Oh my god, I have a schizophrenia tamagotchi."

In keeping with that nineties kid theme (though a friend did recall the game I'd mentioned, on a different platform), I later described Farrrah with a comparison to the golden retriever puppies in Lisa Frank products. She wasn't very cartoony, if a little poorly rendered, but it gave a quick image translated to a more realistic looking hallucination, the chubby, fluffy golden retriever puppy.

Unlike the tamagotchi, I couldn't really decide what Farrah did when she was in that void. She didn't do much. Sometimes I got a flash of her rolling around or chewing on a blurry toy, fading into that space as the real room faded away. When she came into my actual environment, at the most random of moments, she responded to what I did, but not how I willed it. She cowered behind a shelf when my fiancee spoke loudly, and growled at the cats playfully; she might sniff the air and take a step forward curiously if I beckoned, in my mind or in reality, but she still didn't get close enough to see if the tactile hallucinations would line up.

Like some recent others, I could feel her, but she simultaneously appeared several feet away. Still getting used to the tactile hallucinations, it was interesting to note the disconnect. The very occasional auditory hallucination of a yip or growl did seem in line though.

I knew she wasn't real—no running cats or confused people, too many things not quite right— but the responsiveness was interesting. Imperfect and inconsistent, but there, like a dream.

Mostly Farrah was cute, shy, and playful. The only disconcerting thing about the photo calendar ready puppy was that she wasn't quite right, wasn't quite real.

THE PROTECTION OF A FACADE

There are ups and downs to trying hard to appear normal (whatever that may mean). One downside is that it's easy to convince even yourself that nothing is wrong, if you look in the mirror and all looks well. Especially if the facade thoroughly convinces others, who voice that very thought. It's easy to think you're exaggerating or lying even to yourself, especially when you have a real disorder that skews reality just like that.

A thing about schizophrenia is that it sets you in the frame of mind of questioning things. Reality gets tricky easily. Maybe one hallucination is obvious, but you know there are others that aren't. When something is real, and you do think it's real, but in any way off, you still give it a close examination in skepticism. One thing out of place sets off a spiral of—well, if that's maybe not real, what else am I missing? Knowing you see things that aren't there means you question the things that are—always.

I've speculated that the reason I have so many lucid dreams compared to many people I know is because the key to lucid dreaming, according to most how tos, is reality checking. Looking for something out of place enough you realize you're in a dream, and that you can control dreams. You have to set that habit in the waking hours for it to occur to you in a dream, though. And I'm used to doing that in my life so much that it slips into my dreams.

The same goes for mental constructs. You know that you get on the wrong thought trains, delusions, and if you're thinking about having schizophrenia itself, you question that thought train, too, especially when the evidence you're more sure of looks so... normal.

On the upside, it means that unless I'm having a really bad day, when I want to play it down, I can, and when I want to not talk about it, I don't have to. I'm very open about my schizophrenia and pretty much everything else in my life, very out about all of my identities, but I also feel lucky to frequently be able to pass as neurotypical, because the stigma around psychosis and mental illness is very real.

Sometimes I want people to look at me and *wonder*, but not pin me down as psychotic immediately. To be somewhere on the spectrum where I am validated in my illness, but not obvious and discriminated against or worried about. Sometimes I want people to be able to look at me and *maybe* see the psychosis—but see the rest of me, too. And being known as having a psychotic disorder frequently overshadows everything else.

This does mean a bit of an obsession with maintaining those appearances, in various forms. Physical presentation standards—and the ability to keep that up even when there are hard days. I wear only one outfit, the same thing every day, carefully chosen. When I fear I'm slipping mentally, I develop another cycle of particular obsession with making sure my clothes are clean, in good repair, sized appropriately, not too eye catching. The same ideas extend to all parts of my appearance, to my online presence, and to my small mannerisms. And I'm not always able to keep the appearance up—though I've improved with time.

Recently, before a video chat with my therapist, I asked my fiancee to help me trim my bangs so I could actually see my therapist and not the backside of my own hair, and an observing friend said something like, "So, 'I had a psychotic break, but not so much I couldn't get my bangs trimmed.'"

And on the one hand, I wanted to be able to see, and on the other hand… well, yes.

In some ways, I talk about my mental illnesses very openly. There are few cases where I won't mention the diagnosis itself. There are a lot more cases where I play down how troubling it is, or laugh it off. Most of my friends know I hallucinate, but they hear about the flashes of light and the white noise and the echoes and the objects that get flipped in my vision, and less about the corpses and voices. More still hearing random things while wearing noise cancelling headphones, and less sleeping on the couch because beds are a trigger.

It's been a hell of a year (tomorrow) since the PTSD began and brought a fresh wave of psychosis with it. It had been fairly easy for quite a while, before, to live with and ignore the odd white noise or flash of light, and easy to sink into the comfort of maladaptive style daydreaming. After, there were the night terrors that we mistook as seizures, the waking hours' blurred line between flashback and hallucination that eventually leant far towards the latter.

Those are the pieces I try to keep to discussing only within the right context for it, and those are the pieces I can tuck away when I'm able to *look* normal.

If I didn't keep up those appearances—the question of the full extent of illness would come up a lot more, whether I wanted it to or not—something that's hard, mixed with my own trauma, and external stigma and worry—more for the psychosis than for any other condition I have.

So I understand the idea of the facade protecting you.

It's a little wall between you and the possibility of never being able to have a (seemingly) normal moment.

ON FARRAH AND TREATMENT

I swore when my shoulder cramped, which was interesting, because I'd kind of assumed I was nonverbal at the moment, based on the way my thoughts flowed, or didn't, and a familiar feeling somewhere in my throat, though I hadn't tested it.

I couldn't blame my shoulder for cramping; my disorientation at speaking came with the realization that I'd been lying on my office floor staring at the very bottom of my bookshelves again.

Against my back, I felt Farrah, my recurring puppy hallucination, slump, and heard her whimper for attention, wet nose near my neck. The theme of the morning's tactile hallucinations seemed to be—weight. Farrah's dense little body in my hands, slumping against my back in the same manner the cats did, cold paws pressing at spots on my lap.

Just to spite my saying to my therapist yesterday that the tactile and visual hallucinations didn't line up and Farrah teleported away if I tried to get close, the hallucinations started to line up, and she started wanting to cuddle.

She'd been clingy all morning, and while she didn't talk, I felt or knew her thoughts in a way that was hard to explain—the way you knew the facts in dreams that were never presented in a sensory manner. She was disheartened by my therapy video chat yesterday that came to the conclusion—I might need to go back on meds. Probably, in fact.

I'm not trying to get rid of you, was what I thought at Farrah, because this was stupid. She wasn't real, and so wasn't sad that I was trying to stop seeing her—and honestly, she was the least of my issues I was trying to stop seeing. Her behavior was just the manifestation of my own mixed feelings about likely going back on meds.

My old psychiatrist's office wasn't open on weekends, though, and there were no calls to be made just yet. So Farrah—claws pattering on the hardwood and somersaulting clumsily down the stairs and getting stuck in the legs of my desk and trying to eat the real cats' food—kept me company all morning and into the afternoon.

I found myself editing a picture I'd found online that kind of looked like her, to get the image closer to right, as if trying to appease her—*see, you're not going away, you can live in a picture, I can still know what you look like, even if it's in a healthier format.*

I also have developed a bit of an obsession with where Farrah came from. I only have two specific recurring hallucinations currently; one is straight out of a PTSD flashback; I'm very aware of where it came from. The other is Farrah. Any others are not coherent enough to be called recurring. Those little imaginary flashes of light, flips of still objects, white noise I can't pin down.

The only real dog I see regularly looks, sounds, feels, and acts nothing like Farrah. I can't figure out if Farrah is my mental manifestation of *dog* or *puppy* or *golden retriever* or… what word my brain might have decided to attach to, that conjured this particular image. I'm not much of a dog person; that's why my two real pets are cats. Google told me what Farrah meant—I know no real Farrahs and have no personal associations with the name, its origin in a language I don't speak. I keep staring her down, thinking: *Why are you here?*

I get at most a wag of the tail or a yip back.

It's a big question for a little puppy that's not even real.

Talking about it in therapy was strangely disheartening to me, too, because those closest to me are very used to the quirks of my physical and mental health, or at least know reacting strongly isn't going to change it. I forget how concerning certain things sound to the average person, and I'd been out of touch with my therapist for a bit there, when I'd been doing well.

Also disheartening was the fact that, as my psychosis spikes up again, my therapist, an MFT, is not really qualified to treat it. Therapy is not the front line treatment for schizophrenia as it is—medication is. It's an issue we've discussed before. I used to have a second therapist, the psychologist who initially diagnosed me, who my therapist referred me to shortly after I started seeing her in 2015, but the psychologist sadly passed on less than a year later, and I haven't had that second person to treat that side of my illness since.

I can write up new medical files and go back to meditation and read more psychology books and call my psychiatrist and go to my current therapist and do some therapy workbook activities and all, and I have— but having a qualified professional to talk to is a good resource.

But, hard to find. The only name my therapist came

up with off the top of her head to bring in didn't take my insurance. I've had many nightmare therapists and I've had many who were good people who admitted they were in over their heads. The web told me that my old psychologist, the one who passed four years ago, is currently accepting new patients.

The only real thing to do is maintain routines and wait, and wonder if it would work if I carried clumsy Farrah down the stairs.

KNOWING YOUR MIND IS VULNERABLE, AND WHAT YOU DO ABOUT IT

I'm writing. It's going really well. Pages and pages of ink in my beloved dot grid Moleskine. So many pages, I think to comment to friends about my comparatively unpretentious but equally beloved Bic pen that has somehow lasted me almost sixty total pages, plus about half of my previous Moleskine, and months of Word of the Day Post It notes, mailed letters, and other miscellany. I included a picture of the inside of the front cover of my notebook, a gift from my fiancee, with that inside cover inscribed by her at the spot we met on the second anniversary of it, a callback to our first conversation—notebooks.

I write; I take a break to clean a few things when my back complains about sitting. I end up sitting on the bed and reading *Writers on Writing,* a New York Times essay compilation recommended from a workshop class. I go back to writing at my desk. It flows. Something else I can't place my finger on keeps catching my attention. I put noise canceling headphones on that I'm borrowing from my fiancee, with a bit of *Harry Potter* themed ASMR with splashing water and bubbles. I remember putting them on and realizing how much white noise was in my brain for the first time as hallucinations worsened. Something keeps drawing my eyes. I think it's black —a prominent color in my most terrifying recurring hallucination, but it's not that—yet, at least.

Maybe it's the cat. Our fanged black cat naps on the bed. But every time my eyes dart to her, she's still, not eye catching. The legs of my desk, the fabric drawers, my space heater, my knee socks, my desk chair, my computer screen fully dimmed since I'm just using the device for the ASMR—something black. It keeps coming in the corner of my eye. I turn on my task lamp, also black, but hoping the light will dispel some shadows. The other cat, a tortoiseshell, naps in the rope hammock swing, encased in my white canopy and starry string lights.

My fiancee comes and asks if I want anything downstairs while she's going. More black in the corner of my eye at first—her usual attire. I do a double take. No, she's there. Water, I say.

I get the words down a little faster, not sure how much longer they're coming for. I'm behind on words for Camp NaNoWriMo, hoping for my tenth win of 50,000 words or more in a month—one past win being the 100 pages for the sister event for scripts—and I'm not sure yet how many words are actually on the page without the convenience of a computer's word counter, having not typed them up. There are plenty of words crossed out for better ones, and random notes about the story or about things to add to the shopping list, places my handwriting ceases to know what a space is. If I don't write now, with the first signs of my mind fading for a while, I'm probably not going to anymore today.

She comes back with the water and leaves. The cat goes off to explore.

I wish my hands moved faster or my characters got to the point faster. "I'm rambling," one of the characters confesses. *Yes, you are,* I think at her, hands twitching. The black cloud seems to be flashing in and out faster. I should just write down a summary of the rest of this scene in case I don't get to it. The chapter outline lives on my computer, a picture of my whiteboard and some added notes, but it's missing snippets of dialogue and action that have just come to me as I approach them. I add more notes; I can't seem to hold them in my head well anyway. I sense humanoid movement, which means it's probably heading down the PTSD road; I keep seeing it in the mirrored closet doors next to my desk; I have that distinct sense of something behind me and turning around clears it for only a moment.

It's strange to worry about not being able to think. Day to day, it means not holding where this scene is going only in my head, just in case my mind goes mostly out for a few hours and comes back without those ideas. It means a bit of an obsession with certain paperwork.

To be fair, reading *Five Days at Memorial* would give anyone an obsession with living wills, and I've gone and succeeded pro se in probate court with no will recently enough to have it in mind. Those aren't really the papers I'm worried about yet.

Right now, it's mostly a piece of paper in the back of my notebook, my little "SHTF" paper. The sort of things I wish I had written down before the blur of my one abrupt psych ward stay, when I'd abandoned having such a note for a while. Emergency contacts. Basics.

Cat—a black blob in the bed—no, she's on the carpet now—the blob flickers out. I glare at where it was, mostly over knowing I can't see my psychiatrist for over three weeks to keep it flickered out.

I called my psychiatrist first thing Monday morning after I committed to calling, because I'm psychotic but not irresponsible—fear of irresponsibility due to my mind fading out perhaps fueling those papers and other things.

I put the appointment on one of my multiple Google Calendars. My fiancee once said I run my life like I'm a startup CEO rather than a housewife writer with some real estate. I might just be paranoid. She agrees to drive me to the appointment, if it's not on Zoom. I don't drive and while I keep tossing the idea around, I don't want to one day swerve around a dog that isn't there, like the one that accompanied me on my walk the other day, holding an also hallucinated leash in her mouth as she trotted next to me like it was helpful, flickering and then fading entirely by the time I got halfway to my destination.

My therapist has had no luck finding me someone who knows more about psychosis on the therapy side, while I wait on meds, and neither have I. She says the laws apparently changed, according to a coworker of hers, and she's allowed to treat it now, but no more knowledge qualified than she was before. I'm waiting on some books, library and mail order, my finds and my therapist's, and enjoying JSTOR's pandemic discounts, if research is only a grab in the dark for that responsibility and control. One book I'm waiting on is *My Month of Madness*—a paranoid long shot for usefulness, but autoimmune has definitely been thrown around before, and after months of pain turned out to be a rare manifestation of toxic black mold poisoning once, I try to not dismiss rare diagnoses out of hand. Yet I don't want to fall into the "letting WebMD convince you that you have a brain tumor" trap.

So honestly, I am mostly still at waiting, which is a lot of what treatment is. You'd think I'd be better at it by now. Waiting for the black blobs to get too consuming, waiting for my appointment, waiting for books.

I have many virtues, but patience and sanity are not among them.

FUNCTIONALITY THRESHOLDS AND MEDICATION

So I saw a psychiatrist through an online urgent care service after remembering that it was an option, and started on a new antipsychotic.

I had a lot of mixed feelings about going back on meds. At first, I felt like it was a cynical move—the action that confirmed the thought that I wouldn't get better without meds, that I was dependent on them again, that I was worse now than I was back when I got off of them or at any point in between.

Then I started to look at it a little differently.

When I got off the meds, I wasn't working, in school, volunteering, being a great housewife, or honestly being productive at much of anything. My standards for *functional* were a lot lower.

I think what's happening now is more that I've hit a threshold. I have a lot more things I want to do now.

I'm deep into multiple writing and other creative projects (I recently won Camp NaNoWriMo with writing over 50,000 words in July), I read several times as much, I happily handle nearly all of the domestic responsibilities,

I take classes now and then, I do property management and investing, I go on walks, and when there's not a pandemic, I volunteer at the library once a week.

I think that if I wanted to do what I was doing when I got off of meds, I absolutely still wouldn't need the meds.

But I want to be doing a lot more—and I've hit a ceiling. I can't do all the things I want to do now without the assistance of meds.

It is less that my abilities are that much worse and more that they are being pushed for so much more.

So I've had almost a week on the new med. It knocks me out at night; I sleep like the dead for now. I had thought my sleep had been largely okay for a while, but it seems the quality was lacking in a way I couldn't measure, because during the day, I comparatively have so much energy now I find myself confused on what to do with it. I dissociate much less and less strongly, and haven't had a super noticeable hallucination since I started.

So I finished Camp NaNoWriMo, then wrote some more. I started reading several new books, including some on AirBnB management. I got back to crocheting; I socialized; I got the house in shape; I experimented with my new instant camera.

I feel much better about the med decision.

SANITY, OR WRITING?

I get an idea.

A few minutes later, the very distinct thought: *I need to stop thinking about this too hard. Or I need a pen.*

My fingers twitch.

Pen.

It can't move fast enough on the page, chaos that will be a brief note in a dated, tagged table of contents.

Tucked in the back pocket of that notebook that is rarely far from me is a sheet of paper with emergency information about me on it.

In a previous draft, one of the notes, the sort that's more for psych ward intake than found unconscious in a park, noted a few topics that tend to make my condition worse. Absurdist jokes about reality; things like *The Matrix* or *Inception*; general death and gore; certain corners of politics.

The immediately following note said that I might bring these up first—some of them even extremely frequently; I spent years talking about nothing other than gory Hunger Games fanfiction—but to tread with caution. And that I especially bring them up in writing.

It can be hard to find a balance between reality and fiction when you have a condition that heavily blurs those lines to begin with, and the mind and overactive imagination of a writer. I have never been one to write much fluff and happy endings; I write about apocalypses and dystopia, morally gray villain protagonists, death and torture, gore to disturb horror fans, extreme mind and power games, toxic and abusive relationships, manipulation and gaslighting. The note also recommended *don't look in the notebook.* More so a *you're responsible for what you find.* I've read that such dark obsessions can be common for people with PTSD, another factor here.

Yet in reality, the stray comment that is innocently just incorrect can send me into a frantic spiral of questioning what exists.

So, yes, *I need to stop thinking about this too hard. Or I need a pen.*

Frequently, when I question whether something I do, think, or feel, is normal, there are two people I ask. One, my fiancee, who works in STEM and barely even reads fiction, is usually at one extreme of the answer spectrum, while I am at the other. In the middle is my best friend, a writer and reader in much the same genres I am. The overactive imagination of a writer gets them halfway to my end of the spectrum, but psychosis takes me the rest of the way.

Asking about daydreams, my end of the spectrum was, "The room disappears basically entirely. I am now seeing and hearing my characters like I'm exclusively in the room they're in, in detail. I can experience things through their senses. It may or may not be 'pleasant'. It's all a little bit my doing and a little bit theirs. I'm dissociating. It is frequently hard to snap out of."

My fiancee's end of the spectrum was, "I am thinking

about an unrealistic idea with less logic and more fancifulness." I understood that and did that myself sometimes, but it wasn't what I meant by daydreaming, and her version never really went further than what she described.

In the middle was, "I kind of see a picture in picture window of my characters doing things; I can hear it; they might be doing well or bad emotionally; I basically control it. Sometimes I'm a little spacey after." I sometimes, but less frequently, experienced that version, but again, for them it never went further, and for me, it still wasn't what I called a daydream.

Since I have started taking meds again, I have had an easier time slipping out of daydreams, their grip on me less tight, less emotional. The rest is still true. But for a few days as the med levels stabled out in my body, the daydreams were almost hard to stay *in* when I wanted to —and I found that, deeply affected by psychosis or not, they're a very important part of my writing process and I missed them. I felt, strangely, like losing that intensity to the daydreams was to lose touch with my characters, which felt like losing touch with not only writing goals but also good friends. (Now, whether or not most of my characters are good *people* is a very different question).

I was glad when I was again able to stay in them, but a little more at will.

I've written before—and God knows I'm not the only one—about the relations between writers and creativity and mental illness. Most talked about, though, are anxiety and mood disorders, and certainly substance abuse. Psychosis, and especially schizophrenia, seem, while frequently pondered, less well factually documented.

It's something I'd like to look into more in the future.

22

ASSORTED ILLNESSES AND LANGUAGE (A CONLANG CONCEPT)

As someone into grammar and linguistics, who debates the requirements of a split infinitive and the correctness of implied antecedents and whether you can punctuate dialogue with semicolons, for fun, language is in my head a lot.

As someone with schizophrenia, not to mention autism, language gets messy.

I've pondered making a mini conlang based on superlatives.

Tired, tireder, tiredest.

The thing is that the difference between "tired" or "very tired" or "sleepy" or "exhausted" can mean very different things to lots of people.

To me, "exhausted" clearly meant, "I am about to fall asleep on my feet and it is hazardous for me to stand up." I found out that apparently, other people use exhausted to mean what I call pretty sleepy—a strong urge towards going to bed as things got hazy.

Additionally, I separated mental and physical energy in a way a lot of people apparently do not. I can be ready for a long, productive writing session while barely able to sit up. Much less frequently, on the other side, I can be nonverbal and ready to run a mile. Their correlation is low if not nonexistent.

Plus, it can be hard to describe things that are incredibly subjective or an uncommon experience. How dissociated are you? How intrusive are the hallucinations? How bad is the sensory overload? This isn't a new problem—say, pain—if you've ever been to a doctor's office, you've seen a chart of smiley faces and numbers desperately trying to solve it.

So I pondered a sort of mini loglang that would use some extremely simple ways to describe certain spectrums, to be used between me and people its relevant to. I faced the reality that they would go "which one was that word again?" and I would tell them the definition, which meant I should just start with that definition. It still might be useful for journaling or something, and it's still in my mind.

Say, tired, tireder, tiredest, sleepy, exhausted, mental and physical energy.

It could be given a rating system, maybe 1-5.

MentalTired1—messing up a few words now and then, a bit slow to catch hidden meaning or jokes, not coming up with brilliant ideas.

to

MentalTired5—nonverbal, and non responsive to language input.

or

PhysicalTired1—notable muscle fatigue, depending on cause, might be slightly short of breath/sweating.

to

PhysicalTired5—it is hazardous for me to be sitting up unsupported; will be unconscious shortly.

Etc.

There's also the kinds of overlap—mental distress that creates physical symptoms. Anxiety and muscle tension, nausea, chest pain. Depression and lethargy. Hallucinating and dizziness. Sensory overload and headache. Things that can be hard to explain in English if you have only ever experienced the symptoms independently, or only the physical side.

When tested for diagnosis, I took an IQ test, which I don't find to be the one true measure of intelligence or all of what it's sometimes made out to be, but it was interesting, and an example here—

My verbal reasoning? 130.

My spatial reasoning? 92.

I've written millions of words of fiction in my life, never gotten a B in English, but I both miss doorways for walls and still have to do the L thing with my hands to find left and right on a daily basis.

The difference between skills like that also influences how some days I can write a book but not sit up.

When those physical and mental lines get blurry and when adjectives don't describe symptoms, language gets tricky. At least English—I may have to look into others.

What seems like a long time ago, I pondered going into a very specific form of being a therapist as a career based on what I would call conlang therapy—like art therapy, but creating with language. While being a mental health professional is not for me, and I have no idea if that as a therapy type would've been really feasible, it was an interesting concept.

Words make people feel powerful. It's why we reclaim slurs, cling to favorite quotes and lyrics, wear some labels with pride.

Surely there's something to a therapy practice of building yourself up by making language that has failed you, work for you.

Just a thought.

"ARE YOU HALLUCINATING?"

"Are you hallucinating?"

It sounds like such a simple and important question. But there are several catches that people don't realize when they want to hear *yes* or *no.*

First question: do I *know* I'm hallucinating? I usually have a pretty decent grasp on that for the big stuff, but not everyone does. Corpse, not there. Dog I don't have, not there. Hallucinations.

But is that flash of light in the corner of my eye from traffic out the window, or my own mind? Is it just a trick of the light? Is staring at a trick of the light unsurely for way too long a *hallucination?*

What about changing real objects? Is that cup upside down on the counter, or right side up? Well, if I just confirm: *is there a glass*? That's not useful. Sometimes it is *Alice in Wonderland* like distortions, larger, smaller, some more subtle than others until your fingers flit through the top of an object that doesn't quite reach there.

Is there a slight aura around that lamp, or just me? Is the cat messing around upstairs making hard to describe noises, or is it in my head? Neighbors talking indistinctly, or just me?

Should I start describing everything in the room to you to make sure we see all the same things? Hear? Smell?

What about the fact that my sensory processing issues mean I frequently hear very real sounds that other people don't pick up on until they really listen for them? What then?

I remember in a bad psychosis phase putting on noise canceling headphones and realizing how much *noise* I still heard. But it was just that: noise. Like a white noise machine. Like very steady running water. Like the sound of a crowded restaurant when no table is drawing attention in particular. Like the cats making a ruckus upstairs. It just kind of added mental decibels to what was really going on around me (which, as someone with sound sensitivity, is its own very real issue). But how to describe that?

Also consider that my line between reality and hallucination, or even fantasy, is jagged and thin and I'm highly suggestible in that way. If you say, "Are you seeing Farrah right now?" Well, I wasn't. Until you said her name. Now I kind of got a flash of her, my little recurring golden retriever, like a mental flashback. But is that the normal helpless visualization that comes from people talking? What if, three minutes after you said that, she hasn't quite gone away yet, flickering in and out, under a real chair in the room? "Ah, now I am. Nope, not anymore—wait, there it is! Oh—nope. Hold on—ah, there—no."

Is my daydreaming over the line of hallucinating when it sometimes slips a few seconds ahead of my actual thoughts? When characters can do things *unexpected*? When I can't snap back out of it?

Is seeing a blur out of the corner of my eye that's never there when I turn a *hallucination*? Is it a hallucination if

I *sense* something that isn't there, but don't strictly see it?

What if the real issue is delusion—times I *think* I'm hallucinating something that's very much there—like the person asking the question?

"Are you hallucinating?" It's not really a yes or no question. *No* is a simple, soothing answer, if temporary by nature. *Yes* means something definable has gone wrong without doubt. But it's not really *hallucinating* or *not hallucinating*—or, for my *Hunger Games* fans—*real* or *not real.*

The answer for me, sometimes, is pretty definitively yes. But I'm not sure I'd ever give a *definitive* no—because what do I know? Who am I, the schizophrenic one, to answer that? I don't trust my perceptions any longer. And how long do you have to think you're not hallucinating for before it counts? If Farrah was here three minutes ago and isn't now, can I say no? An hour? A day? A week? Ah, gerunds.

I don't really have a better question to propose. Just some things to keep in mind. It's tricky in a lot of often overlooked ways. That's the thing with schizophrenia —it's not a *real or not real* game—even when it is mostly episodic, you are *always* questioning. Every flash of light, every distant conversation, every dog, every bump in the night.

Real or not real?

Might want to ask someone else.

FLASH MEMOIRS FROM MY NOTEBOOK IN 2020

I started to worry about living today.

I was worried before about surviving.

Food.

When will it run out? Where will it come from? At what cost? At what risk? For how long? Who will it feed?

Water. Soap. Medicine. Toiletries.

Today…

Will I pretend everything is okay enough that I can write? Read? Crochet? Make a font, make something fun to eat?

Even some of the worst apocalypse novels are told via diary.

What if I run out of yarn and electricity and paper and pens and books?

Before I run out of food?

I dream about Dad a lot, dead or alive.

It's not usually really him, if dead.

Sometimes it's Mom.

Sometimes it's Grandma.

I think about the email he sent my mom about fleeing, about the box in his garage with outdated first aid gear.

And he said, "It's irresponsible not to be prepared," about living and dying both but—

Bold words from a man who died without a will.

Sometimes Dad's alive in my dreams but I know he's not; sometimes I dream about the grief itself.

I fall asleep in my bed; I wake up standing next to the body again.

I zone out in my room, snap out of it in a flashback, standing next to the body again.

Standing next to the body again.

And again.

How do I tell Mom I'm finally starting to fall asleep with my eyes closed, that I jump just as much when startled but I've never screamed, that when I blink in daylight it's usually okay, that white linens aren't as frightening now, that I went into the bedroom while my girlfriend was sleeping without thinking, that I don't sleep on the couch as much?

If I talk about getting better, she'll say the same, "It should've been me," and I'll say:

"That's a noble game," or, "But it wasn't," or, "But I'm glad it wasn't," or, "No, Mom, it really shouldn't have been you."

Mom's never seen me cry over it and she's not going to.

I'm still trying to think my way out of that room.

There's a dead bird I've passed on my walk at the curb for

a few days now and I keep thinking I'll walk the other
way or not look and then I don't, and it's decaying into
liquid, decaying, decaying, and I think of Dad, and how I
thought I wouldn't sit with Grandma's body, either.

Morning. It's sun warmed, bright, sunlight patches on
light carpet, sunbathing cats, warm fur, stretch, purr,
yawn. Smells like sunlight on light dust. Sun, sun, sun.

My walk—everyone else is in pairs—you can tell who
dragged whom. It's almost cold out. Crisp. Fresh. No hot
pavement scent yet.

Brunch. Clear glass bowls of chopped fruit still wet
from washing. A few flowers remain alive in the vase.
Stripes of sun through the blinds on the tablecloth. Sweet
strawberries and Nutella, the crunch of toast. My best
friend is bedheaded and in pajamas. My wife to be is
dressed in black. We all talk and laugh too much and too
loud.

My fiancee and I cook dinner together. Evening slats of
sun. The broiler, the frying, the oven, the stove—hum. It's
hot. Everything smells delicious. She is so beautiful. The
potatoes are colorful, the pork chops shaping up to the
right hue.

Today's the kind of mental health day where you listen
to Evanescence and hope for the best. Time and space
happen to me strangely.

It's 9:30 AM and I'm nonverbal, and it feels like I
shouldn't be—it's too early, too much of a problem.

Nonverbal, like drunk, happens at more like dinner. But I woke up like this, and I don't drink.

My dearest fiancee,
    It is May 2020.
    The world is ending.
    And you have asked me to marry you.

It's late afternoon, hot, dry, the sun just starting to cast long shadows. The pool water is cool and clear, has to be eased into, but refreshing. Mom is drinking white wine out of a Dixie coffee cup. All of the neighbors are in their pools too, cannonballs and voices carrying over. My mom and my best friend and my fiancee and I splash each other, blow water through pool noodles, throw a ball around. Everything smells a little like chlorine. My fiancee and I lay on the bed in the afternoon and cuddled and talked about the future earlier. Later, we all eat dinner still a little wet, but in dry clothes, and pick at desserts knowing we'll sleep well. All the people I love are happy. We talk about the engagement. The AC isn't too cold. The food is good and plentiful. I stepped out of the pool and started dinner wet and still in my underwear. And life is good.

I have started to hallucinate a golden retriever puppy regularly. Her name is Farrah.

The smell of heat on pavement. Sweat. Water getting warm in bottles. Swings creaking. Gas station snacks eaten on the side of the parking lot in a patch of shade. Kids yell in the distance. My best friend's voice. The chime of the gas station door opening and closing.

I woke up from my first dream where people were just…
wearing masks. How weird is it to adjust?

I wake trying to scream and batting at a corpse that isn't
there.

The Christmas tree with rainbow lights. Wrapping
paper, stockings, pillows, blankets—everywhere. The
fireplace is on. Games and snacks line the table, brunch
abandoned. Instrumental Christmas music plays. I lie
in the pile of wrapping paper and blankets wearing my
Santa dress, head on a bathrobe gift, my wife next to me,
my best friend next to her. We laugh. Mom is close by. I'm
home. It's Christmas morning.

THE NOTEBOOK UNIVERSE (DELUSION)

My wife and I went to the dentist recently (a thrilling start to any story, I know). I was just in for a routine cleaning, her for the first of a series of more involved appointments. But that day was just an exam for her, and, finished before I was, she sat near me and made small talk with the hygienist while I made garbled sounds around the vacuum, water, and polishing tools.

At some point, while I was—understandably—distracted, she had an idea, and, with nothing else to write on, jotted it down in the back of my nearby notebook, sitting with my things on the counter.

But I didn't notice this.

Flash forward a few days, and I—somehow for the first time—noticed the note. A mundane investment strategy to look into.

The thing was that I didn't write it. Or I didn't remember it. But there it was, in my notebook, in my pen's ink. Not in my usual handwriting, I was pretty sure.

And reality broke.

I showed it to her. "I can't remember writing this," I

kept saying, distressed, convinced I had left myself a note
I had no recollection of. It was not on my next page in
line, it wasn't dated, the page wasn't numbered, it wasn't
in my table of contents; at the moment, it just made no
sense to me.

A friend was over; I was just with it enough to insist
we didn't have this conversation in front of him. We
didn't.

She thought at first that perhaps I was upset
she'd used my notebook without asking. But she
grasped quickly that this wasn't a roundabout way of
communicating I was upset; reality was just broken by
the surprise, something that occasionally breaks my
concept of *real.* The unexpected twist in reality. I had no
problem with her using my notebook.

She explained that she had written it. Several times.
The dentist's office story. But I couldn't grasp this. My
mind was already off in the alternate universe it was
building without me to explain this, while ignoring all
easier logic. In this reality, everyone had Their Notebook.
Like you had fingerprints or a social security number.
And only *you* could write in your notebook. I don't know
how this formed or why this made more sense than her
borrowing mine. But in this world, this meant that she
had to have written this note in *her* notebook, but, due
to our deep connection or legal marriage or something,
her notebook had, in a way, "hacked" my notebook
psychically, transporting notes between them.

That wasn't so bad, but my mind was spinning with
possibilities. Did that mean that *anyone* could get into
my notebook from a distance? I didn't want literally
anyone in my notes.

And I was off investigating locks and privacy measures

(which apparently stopped psychic transports). She let me.

Reality slowly returned as I tried to focus enough to make sense of Amazon reviews.

(In the end, I did decide that a bit of security—against real dangers—wasn't my worst idea, and got a fire and water proof accordion style folder—a type I'd been considering using sometimes for my notebook and pen and loose papers anyway. We already have a fireproof safe for important documents, but nothing portable.)

So went the notebook universe. Would've been a cool story premise. (I did end up writing about a non magical stolen notebook shortly after, this time about an existing character with actual privacy concerns.)

But, thankfully, I grasped within hours that the premise wasn't reality.

And so episodes go.

THE STORIES WE TELL OURSELVES: NARRATIVES, TRAUMA, AND MY CHILDHOOD DOG

My wife told me that her version of the story starts here:

We're sitting in the car, driving to my dad's house. We're passing the Walmart and the AC is fighting the Vegas heat, the stifling air quality two days after the Fourth of July. She takes my hand. "I'm sure it's fine," she says, then grimaces. This is a validating *aha* moment for me at the time—she has doubts. Later, she says she regretted the words the moment they were out of her mouth. *But what if it's* not *fine?*

But for me, the story doesn't start in the car.

As a writer, I like to start in the height of the action—I would open this story with me standing over the body.

But that's not where my real version of the story starts. The one I tell myself on long walks and long nights like a lullaby.

No; the story starts with Ziva.

Ziva came to me as an awkward looking Dutch Shepherd puppy as I was finishing the fifth grade and embarking on the terrifying journey that is middle school.

She stayed with me through panic attacks and psychosis, self harm and delusion, lost chances and bad breakups, my parents' divorce and leaving school several times over.

When I'd attempted suicide at seventeen, my best friend's mom, a psychiatrist, told me I had to hang in there because Ziva would never understand why I left her.

So I hung in there.

Ziva, however, passed in the spring of 2019. I had a lot more, or understood I had a lot more, to *hang in there* for by then, and hadn't felt like I'd been *just hanging in there* for years; no cutting, no attempts. I was in the relationship of my dreams and surrounded by people who loved me.

But one morning, a few months later, Ziva came back to me in a dream.

In the dream, I was in my childhood home. My dad's house, at the time, in reality. Ziva entered through a burst of white light.

I understood in the dream that she was dead, but in the grips of sleep, believed that she had come back to visit me. She wagged her tail and spun around. I gave her lots of scritches and told her all of the things I could want to say.

But Ziva kept looking back at the white light she'd come from, antsy. Like she was trying to tell me something. Maybe that she had to go again. I let her run back into the light. I woke up.

That morning, it became clear no one had heard from

my dad in some time.

That morning, we were in the car. *"I'm sure it's fine."*

That morning, I stood over the body, and wondered if something in me had already known.

I tell myself the story a lot.

Ziva. The messages with my mom. Why were heat sensitive packages piling up propped against Dad's unopened front door for days? Why had he not put the trash bins down at the curb on trash day? Sitting in the car. Knocking. Using my spare key to open the door. Thinking that I am the only one with a spare key. Mom, now his next door neighbor, was thinking of checking on him when she got back from an errand. I have the key that was hers. Yelling for Dad in a house where I am the only thing living. *"Hey, Dad! Anyone home? Daddy!"* Walking back out, down the stairs, swearing I will not hand the key to anyone else who's not a professional.

"It's not fine," I tell my then-girlfriend, now-wife through the passenger window of her car. She's confused, not having gathered from my demeanor that it's not fine, though I'm not making much sense verbally. *"There's this thing in my dad's bed. It's not my dad. But… I think it used to be."*

I had left the door open behind me, the key more about *blessing* than physical entry. The smell wafts out of the house. She gets it.

Calling my mom. How do I tell her? She is out at lunch with Grandma, on break from considering puppies at an adoption fair. Calling 911. *"No rush, I guess."* Enough firefighters for a calendar, who just keep offering me water while I try not to puke on the lawn. Police, and a report hand written at my mom's kitchen table. What can I say?

I call my best friend in the bathroom. *"My dad's, kinda… dead. I think he's… been dead, for a while now."*

Grandma tells me, *"Oh, Hannah, I just knew something wasn't right. I just knew it wasn't right when he didn't put the trash bins out that week…"*

The coroner. *"You look really young,"* she tells me over and over.

"Twenty-one," I say, unable to think of anything else.

And a counselor who is so high empathy I think she might now be having a worse day than I am.

"First we have to identify him," the coroner is explaining to my mom, as we fill in details.

"You can't just…?"

"It's not… really… a visual thing."

"Well, what about fingerprints?" My mom loves crime shows. She knows how they ID a body at various stages.

"This isn't really…" The coroner is trying to be gentle here. She looks at me, the known witness. *"This isn't really a 'fingerprints' kind of situation. Do you maybe know who his dentist was? For the records?"*

My mom has a white knuckled grip on my hand. The volunteer counselor looks like she might cry.

After the coroner leaves, my mom examines a picture she took of my dad in his youth, in a collage frame in her room. He is victorious, standing on a rock at the end of a long hike, arms thrown to the sky. Yosemite at sunset is the backdrop, their favorite beautiful place, the place they met, lived, worked, and fell in love.

"Cheers," my mom says to the sky, to the picture of Dad, holding up her gluten free beer. Some of Ziva's toys still line her floor.

I think parts of the story have been compromised by time—my private game of telephone. Other parts, by flashbacks, by nightmares, by hallucinations—all blurring the narrative.

Sometimes I try to change it. I don't start with Ziva. I go back to the day my father almost certainly actually died. Ten days earlier. We're sitting on his couch. I'm in the neighborhood to bring in Mom's mail and check on a few plants while she's on a trip with Grandma, pick up a few items I left when I moved out.

I visit with Dad. We sit on his couch. He says he has a headache. We talk about anything. He says he doesn't think that anyone really kills themselves. Evolution wouldn't allow it. Depression is what kills them. The parasite that pulls the trigger—that's not *you.*

But that adds up to the beginning of a very different story.

My father didn't kill himself. I shook the pill bottles on his nightstand, all as full as they come. I looked for a note and found nothing. I found his guns stowed safely in his closet.

No, my father had a heart attack.

And I cannot quite bring myself to tell the story that's not so neat, that has false leads. I always come back to starting with Ziva, with the narratively neat omen.

But that's not how life works.

In one of my writing projects, a character with PTSD seeks and gets a chance to watch video footage of one of the most traumatic events in her life.

It's re-traumatizing to watch, but she's obsessed with what details the following flashbacks, nightmares, time, retellings, and additional trauma have blurred.

When asked if seeing the "truth" made her feel better, she says it's complicated.

I understand that. The sequence is definitely something born of my own emotions.

I wonder what I would do if I had the same opportunity.

Really, I know I could never resist. I know it would be traumatizing all over again. I know my final answer would be *it's complicated*.

Still.

I have three basic PTSD nightmare templates that seem to cycle on a loop, though inconsistently.

In one, we're moving, or buying a rental property. In any case, we're touring a house, sometimes empty, sometimes model home. Either way, there's always a bed in one room with a corpse in it. And it's never addressed in the dream, really. A sigh of, "We'd have to get a biohazard team in again… the ozone machine…" as if we're fixing a plumbing issue.

In another, someone dies, and it's dramatic but often off screen. It's emotion based, a montage of the trauma, grief, and logistics to follow. Pro se probate court and handling of possessions, telling people, paperwork, and the talking, talking, talking. I've been through the process enough. Dad. Later, Grandma, too, lies, lays, all too still in her bedroom, but it's been minutes, not days, and family talks around her.

In the most common dream, though, I'm talking to my dad. Sometimes someone else, but most often him. Sometimes he prods me to remember something. Sometimes, it hits me all on its own. "You're dead,"

I'll remember, often aloud, in the dream. And he'll immediately decay, turning into the ten day old version of his corpse.

I can run down the templates easily. I've done it so often, my best friend had a nightmare identical to the third version, though they never met my father, dead or alive, just heard about a hundred versions of this dream. They woke from it once in the way I've woken from it a hundred times: bolting upright, in a cold sweat, panting, shaking, and desperately trying to scream.

Narrative therapy is supposed to address these stories we tell ourselves. And stories can be therapeutic. After that long, awful day, nausea fading to the realization I'd had only a smoothie that morning, when offered any choice I wanted—*"You found your father's ten day old corpse today. You can pick the restaurant."*—I chose Panera, because that's where I used to go every Tuesday, for the local National Novel Writing Month meetup, to talk and write and eat and get lost in stories like the rest of the week hadn't happened, which always made it feel safe.

And by editing those stories, we edit our outlook.

There's a lot of potential I see here, as a mentally ill writer.

Change the narrator—cue empathy.

Change where it begins—add context.

Change the focus—change the moral of the story.

Change where it "ends"—add hope.

Changing your fate is a common theme in fiction.

I don't feel like the story I tell myself really has an ending. It fades into other thoughts at various points. Probably for the best.

But soon enough, I always find myself back at the

beginning: with Ziva.

TURNING HALLUCINATIONS INTO CHARACTERS: ARE THEY ANY MORE REAL?

She's here again, so I'm not having as okay of a day as I thought.

The backyard is mostly dark, but she's there in the shadows of the bushes, darting or teleporting around. Compared to what I usually see in dark shadows when my mind turns on me? I'll take the puppy.

"Hi, Farrah," I deadpan from the swingset in the AA tone. It *has* been a long day, I guess, and I no longer care if the neighbors can hear me. Still, I take out one headphone, still blaring *Hamilton*, like it matters.

Farrah smiles at me in this way that real dogs don't really *smile,* wags her tail and bounds over, under where I swing. Back through. Again and again. Like she's *trying* to get me to kick her at full speed. She's worse than the little kids at the park. I sigh and, properly distracted, stop swinging.

My darling hallucination races in circles around my feet. A lot of energy for the evening. *What?* I ask her mentally. *You're not a herding dog.* But she wants me inside, much the way the real cats start herding me to the bedroom around this time.

But it doesn't seem to be sleep she wants. I'm determined to sit in the living room and write down an idea I had on the swing before I do anything else. When I do, Farrah settles down. I can *feel* this weird sense of relief on her, like I feel it as my own when I get the idea safely on paper before my mind gives up completely.

I look at my notebook. *This* was what she wanted?

I look back up. She's gone.

All right. I've accepted that Farrah's basically a mirror of my own emotions most of the time, and if everything about her says, "Write *now now now*," then I guess now is the time.

Writing the schizophrenia fiction piece I'm working on is hard at times. There's a lot of *me* in it, even more than in most of my fiction, and in a trippy, intimate way. There's a lot of Farrah in it, too—even more literally. I give her the same role in the schizophrenic main character's life as she has in mine. So now she's not only my *schizophrenia tamagotchi,* but one of my characters.

And my characters, like Farrah, have minds of their own to an extent. Many authors think of it like that, but for me it's even a little more true, I think. My characters jump ahead of me both in plot outlining and in daydreams that slip away from me. I fade into a somewhat omniscient position in their world and often find it hard to come back whether I want to or not. When I do, it's often disorienting, especially if I totally lost track of the real world and snap back abruptly due to the doorbell ringing or dissociation suddenly clearing or such. My world, the real world, goes away entirely, and here I am in theirs, less and less in control the longer I stay in and the emotionally deeper I dive.

It's kind of like Ahtohallan in *Frozen 2*. You can go deeper and deeper into this world of sensations and memories that are not your own. To a point, you can get back out, though the journey back gets longer and longer. After a point, well:

"Dive down deep into her sound
But not too far, or you'll be drowned"

So what does it mean now that Farrah—originally, and, still, a recurring hallucination—is now a character in one of those worlds my mind vanishes to? Does she get to play a double role in my psychosis, not only entering my world—which my characters generally don't— but finding me trapped in one of hers? Is that why she beckoned me to the notebook—like asking me to come home?

Usually, when I write, it's taking something only I can see —the story in my head—and turning it into something other people can read. It's creating—Real from Not Real, in a way. Completely imaginary concepts floating through my brain turn into hundreds of pages I can hold in my hand. It's not making the story *Real,* but making that dreamscape in my head widely accessible, like handing out a key, a map—in the form of a book.

But if I take something as deeply Not Real as Farrah, and give her that quasi Real form… does she become any More Real? What if other people can know Farrah, too —by the power of words on a page? Does that make her less just a quirk of my brain chemicals? Someone saying that they hallucinated Harry Potter, for instance, would be much easier to communicate with than someone hallucinating some boy with round glasses and a lightning shaped scar who could do magic, with seven books' worth of story that only they could see. At that point, we might not share the exact vision of Harry—but I sure have a clue what they're talking about, and the seven years of magic seems a lot saner.

When I write and get feedback, people tell me their thoughts on my characters. They might have a different opinion than me about their moral stances, or a slightly different picture of what they look like. They might even go off and have them in their own daydreams, their own versions of them that don't just follow the script, but are based on their identity more than their role in a plot. People tell me about gasping when my characters are surprised, holding their breath when they're afraid, crying when they're upset, developing crushes on their love interests.

These characters aren't just concepts in my head at that point. They're out there in the world and I can talk about them with other people the way I talk about people I know in real life, or about Harry Potter. It's not uncommon for my wife to walk into a conversation I'm having with my writer best friend and ask, "Wait, are we talking about real people?" (The answer is usually no.)

So what about Farrah? If I make her just as accessible as any character—if others can talk about her like someone they know, or like any known fictional figure—is seeing her saner now? Is her identity something like a socially acceptable shared delusion, when we can both hold the key to her world in our hands?

If she got as popular as Harry Potter? Probably.

MY SCHIZOPHRENIA STORY

When I got my first definitive sign I had a mental illness, I was writing.

I was near the cusp of fourteen and in Algebra I. December 2011. Given some time to do homework or such at the end of class, I, as I often did, took to writing.

I was writing a character death scene in which the character in question drowns. In the ultimate irony, the character in question was schizophrenic—but we won't get there for a while.

The important thing at the time was that I had a near lifelong fear of water. Being a desert dweller, it didn't come up much, but the ocean, especially, or even lakes— drove me into a panic. I had recurring nightmares about tsunamis or storm surges, drowning. (This later turned out to be likely due to my respiratory issues flaring during sleep, pre surgery for them, *causing* the daytime phobia.) In any case, this scene was close to home.

At some point while writing about this character running out of oxygen, I snapped out of my zone and realized that I actually couldn't breathe.

Things went quickly from there. I was rushed to the nurse's office and then to the ER, hyperventilating on the edge of blacking out, vision going dark, limbs too numb to stand, clutching at the chest pain.

I was diagnosed with my first panic attack.

And after the first, they kept coming. Over the summer, I started therapy and medication.

About a year later, I was taking a Biology exam when I started being taunted by red, blobbish, demonic figures drowning images of those I loved—down to my cat—in blood, singsonging gibberish insults.

I began having such episodes as frequently as the "old" panic attacks. I was often delusional—paranoid, physically lashing out at anyone trying to comfort or move me—or catatonic—my arm dropping limply if you lifted it—during.

By spring semester of tenth grade, 2014, it was far too much—especially at this high pressure magnet school— and I left school for a year of "homeschooling" before I was able to get my high school equivalency a year early. I was too agoraphobic to leave the house for a while. It was a critical time for me in many ways. My parents got a divorce. I made my first adult friends—all writers— and got into my first serious relationship. I attempted community college for creative writing and made a few bucks writing clickbait. I volunteered and got involved with NaNoWriMo. Mostly, I wrote.

Parts of what at first seemed like—maybe, at the time, were—isolated episodes, became patterns, habits, and day to day, on a much lower level. Some things, in hindsight, had been with me my whole life. I sought another diagnosis by now, besides the anxiety and schizophrenia—autism. I spent most of a month nearly nonverbal, and was almost hospitalized.

When things got worse, my mood plummeted. For most of 2015, I fell into patterns of self harm and suicidal ideation, or at least the urge to run far away, or sleep for a very long time. I attempted suicide that September, and it was a turning point. I swore off self destructive urges, save a few once off relapses I could count on one hand years apart, and threw myself into change.

In the fall of 2017, I left to attend a private four year liberal arts college in Cambridge, MA. I *loved* the school. I loved the town; I loved the people there; I loved what I was learning. That wasn't the problem.

Being too far from home, maybe, on my own, or meds that needed to be adjusted—whatever it was, I landed in a psych ward—finally, after a lot of near misses, hospitalized for the first time, less than two months into the school year.

I tried to stick it out for a while, going back and forth on my decision, but within a few weeks, landed safely home in Vegas, at a loss for what the future looked like.

Eight days later, I met the love of my life. That changed everything.

Now, the timing, of course, looked horrible. But three years later to the day, 2020, we were married in a ceremony in the beautiful home we own, surrounded by people we love, as people pursuing our passions. I was about to self publish my first book, which would be quickly followed by more, and was soon to start teaching alternative sexuality classes via webinar (within months, I'd also be running a related local group). I was going to start taking a household management course online, and was learning how to be an effective landlord. And, I was a happy housewife who got the girl, the two cats, and the house on the end of the cul de sac.

In the ceremony, our officiant mentioned that we had packed thirty years of marriage into three years of courtship. I almost died of black mold poisoning, all but bedridden for months. I had life changing surgery. Two deaths in my family, and estate handling. We bought a house and moved. A pandemic, quarantine. I went off and then back on meds, though I eventually left therapy. We thought, briefly, my wife might lose her job. There were things with her family. Medical emergencies or surgeries for the cats. Mental and physical health issues. For all the health issues I brought in, I also now had PTSD from one of those family deaths in Summer 2019.

Is everything perfect now? Is everything solved? No, but I'm writing on a laptop in front of me with a warm cat in my lap and my beautiful wife three feet away. The sun is shining; the neighbors' son plays with his dog outside. We saw friends and family yesterday and we will today. I have things to do I can't wait to get to, and a vacation coming up.

And life is pretty good.

TRACKING CONTRIVANCE VS. MY MENTAL HEALTH AT THE TIME

I've been working on my fiction novel, *Contrivance*, since 2011. Numerous drafts, huge changes, shifts of universes, new plots, evolving characters, and total do overs.

My goal here is this: trace those changes along with my mental health state at the time.

(Note: this post was updated to go through the current month, after the original post.)

December 2011

Contrivance is born of a massive *Hunger Games* fan fiction project. I'm now creating the characters who will ultimately become the main characters of *Contrivance,* though, at the time, they're simply original characters to play a background role in the fan fiction, the Gamemakers, who create the titular Death Game, the Hunger Games.

It's the holiday season, and I'm running around town, shopping with my dad. I lean a back to school sale composition notebook on the back of our shopping cart and start on basic character profiles. Pull names from a list I've kept of ideas. Write interactions to test how these characters go together by the fire and Christmas tree at home. Lavender, my eventual main character, currently the Head Gamemaker, already technically exists, but not in any recognizable form.

It's Christmas break of eighth grade. Days before school let out, I had my first panic attack while working on another part this series in free time during Algebra I. Rushed to the nurse's office and then the ER, I went home early that day, took a day or two off, and went back for the last day before break.

These characters catch my interest quickly. By New Year's, I'm on chapter three of the companion story to the series I'm writing that introduces them, distracted from all of life's new questions.

July 2012

I've begun therapy and medication for anxiety. I'm working on a different companion story to that big series. This one introduces Justice as a character (which we won't come back to for a while).

I write an original short story, "Contrivance", using "the Gamemakers", for a summer program for gifted kids, where I basically take a semester of Creative Writing in three weeks at the local university.

The universe concept is that in a world where

everyone is assigned a job by lottery, promising young people get a chance at the best jobs by proving themselves in a VR simulation called Contrivance, which also matches them to the field where they'll do best, personalized testing based on analysis of their dreams, which can be recorded. The short story basically tracks one run of Contrivance the game, taking a few weeks.

A few names and appearances shift with the universe change, suited to something that's not the *Hunger Games'* stylized Capitol. Some don't stick, but the ones I feel the need to change here eventually settle out to something new, among other minor changes. I have to submit two short stories for review over the course of the class. The instructor tells me that the other is good, but "Contrivance" is clearly where my heart is. And maybe it's more than a short story.

April 2013

In January, I had my first psychotic episode, terrifying demonic hallucinations. The episodes keep coming, hallucinations paired with paranoid delusion or catatonia, tears or panic.

I begin writing a novel draft of *Contrivance* for Camp NaNoWriMo, a challenge to write 50,000 words of fiction in one month. I end up writing over 77,000 words that month. It goes from Lavender's job interview for Lead Deviser (the "Head Gamemaker" equivalent) to the completion of the first time she leads Contrivance, about a year later.

I'm permanently stressed and sleep deprived by the magnet school I'm at. In late March, after receiving a poor grade from a spiteful instructor for a special project that halts all normal classes, I panic, knowing it'll be incorporated into my English grade. I ask my English teacher if I can submit a novel I'm writing next month for extra credit. He's a little baffled, but says yes.

In this draft, Lavender inherits my psychosis. It fades in and out in a few more drafts, but mostly doesn't last.

April 2014

I do NaNo two more times in the middle.
In July, I write over 93,000 words, a sequel
to *Contrivance* titled *Trial,* named after a feature of the in universe game. In this one, the Contrivance test takers are kidnapped by rebels, though Lavender teams up with the usually evil Contrivance Director (who oversees the more administrative and financial side of Contrivance) to rescue them. To discourage revolution, Contrivance is toned down a bit.

I've started frequently pairing Lavender and Francisco, one of the Devisers, off at the end, though it's always strangely sudden, and sometimes even in the epilogue, they split up again. It's not quite working.

By April 2014, I'm ready for another draft
of *Contrivance* itself.

A lot of the characters are taking very recognizable shape by now. Not so much a contradiction of what they were before as a solidification. Lavender and Malka still have a long way to go, but their relationship is starting to take on the more formal mentor/apprentice turn. Malka is the former Lead Deviser (the leader of the Devisers, who create Contrivance) and has a lot of advice for her replacement as she steps down, as always. In this draft, there's a formal office mentoring program for new employees; Kaye, hired at the same time as Lavender, is involved as well, though from even the short story, Lavender seems to unofficially look out for her. Here, Lavender and Malka (and Kaye) don't meet before Lavender's job interview, though it's clear Malka's had her eye on Lavender for the role for quite some time as she went through training. (The formal office mentoring program is interesting and sticks around for years, but doesn't make the final cut.)

Meanwhile, my psychosis is getting out of hand, and I leave school, too agoraphobic to leave the house.

July 2014

My parents have gotten a divorce. I'm planning to homeschool in the fall. To overcome my agoraphobia, I've started going to the weekly NaNoWriMo meetups.

In this July's NaNoWriMo, Lavender's hostile relationship with the Contrivance Director (who in previous drafts frequently would do things like use torture just to send a message) comes to a head when the Contrivance Director tortures and plans to kill Kaye, nearby but outside of Contrivance Headquarters, which at this time was an isolated complex in the middle of nowhere. (That setting lasted for quite some time, later shifting to New York for a notable minute, before settling in Washington, DC.)

Lavender and the other Devisers thwart this plan, ending in Lavender killing the Contrivance Director. Realizing that the people inside the complex are not on their side, they flee into the wilderness, hoping to make it to the actual Contrivance Testing Complex to get a hold of the right government officials.

Once they do, Lavender is on trial for voluntary manslaughter, though sentencing gets reduced to probation and fines. Contrivance's staffing gets an overhaul to prevent people like the Contrivance Director from getting in, and the Deviers safely return to Contrivance Headquarters, though Lavender is suspicious of the new, innocent Contrivance Director and doesn't seem to fully recover from all the events, developing severe PTSD.

This turns into a nervous breakdown and she ends up in a psych ward for part of the novel later. Malka is effectively the interim Lead Deviser again, as Lavender's supposed to focus on recovery and not her job (something she struggles with, though she starts to grasp the importance of it).

There were a lot of issues with this draft (see the gaping plot holes), but it got into some interesting themes. We really start to question the Devisers' morality outside of even Contrivance, see mixed factions within the government, and explore a lot more mental health themes.

November 2014

I'm still trying to get the above kind of outline to work, but failing. Most of the plot is eventually scrapped, along with most things to do with the Contrivance Director. I don't finish NaNo. Mostly non verbal for nearly a month due to a mix of dissociation, disorganized thoughts, and distracting hallucinations, I myself almost end up in a psychiatric ward, though in the end I simply commit to sorting out my meds.

February 2015

Writing continues, heavily focused on Lavender and Kaye's friendship. I'm starting to realize that I care more about the Devisers' relationships than about any world or plot issues, but I'm not sure what to do about it.

I develop a self-harm problem. Interestingly, self harm and suicidal ideation are the key mental health issues that plague Kaye. In many early drafts, she commits suicide near the end of the novel/series. (Rissa, another Deviser, frequently does, too. This was in drafts where Malka usually died first of fairly natural causes, resulting in emotional chaos for the Devisers. Rapidly killing off half of the main characters for non plot related reasons was becoming an issue, though.)

September 2015

I've started community college classes, but it's not going well. *I* attempt suicide, an ultimate low point, though it actually turns out to be a key turning point. I swear off self harm and with only a a few relapses in the next several years, quit entirely. I'm also around this time diagnosed with autism, schizophrenia, and anxiety. I'm working on new Contrivance ideas.

November 2015

I finish NaNo again despite a hectic month of family medical issues, though my own are improving, working on *Contrivance*, but exploring new ideas and writing in random orders, not going for a full draft. I've scrapped the job lottery/ability testing idea for worldbuilding issues, and go for general unethical experimentation instead.

Somewhere in here, I know Malka's aged moved up a little, about sixty to about seventy.

In the past year or so, Malka and Lavender's relationship has become increasingly hostile in every draft. Malka seems to no longer be there with just perhaps unnecessarily high standards, but seems to exist to criticize and cause problems. Rather than trying to follow Malka's advice out of respect for her abilities, Lavender seems to be just trying to tread water. Malka especially interferes in Lavender's connection with Kaye.

By the end of the month, I've done my first official experimentation with the idea that there's more history between them than meeting at Lavender's job interview, starting to really roll with the childhood apprentice idea I formerly only entertained as an alternate history.

January 2016

Still in a bit of a low spot, I try a collaboration in which the Devisers go on a quest for the government by travelling between universes to meet with my co-creator's characters, powerful magician sorts working for a military in the other world. The Devisers will bring them modern war technology and strategy in exchange for magical training. It's short lived, but kind of comes back later...

I've started experimenting with the idea that Kaye is autistic, and she occasionally comes into Lavender's new backstory with Malka, though I can't seem to make her stay there. I think this is around the time Malka either developed a military backstory or it really became relevant.

The next month or so, I relapse once on the self harm.

March 2016

I'm improving mentally, but still stuck on what the plot for *Contrivance* actually is, so I take a break from it as a serious original fiction project and throw the characters back into something like fan fiction. I'm wrapping up the fan fiction universe the "Gamemakers"/"Devisers" still do exist in, in their original form, so I try something new.

It's still *kind of* original fiction. The Devisers, doing experiments for the United States government, conduct their most questionable one yet, based on a now old dystopian novel: *The Hunger Games.* Could such a thing really happen? What were the effects on society? How did people just let it be?

I called it *Contrivance Chronicles.* There were actually several more playful, lighter touches here. Justice joins this cast for the first time, though she's not a Deviser. In the fan fiction universe, due to character deaths, two new Gamemakers had joined the panel, Zeely and Laya (who's the sister of one of the Devisers, Thespian, sometimes seen previously as an intern). They both appear in *Contrivance Chronicles* as well, though neither lasted long as Devisers in most original drafts of *Contrivance.* Laya, prominent as Thespian's sister in some drafts, is cut not long before the final version. Another new Deviser named Jorah sometimes appears briefly, though in about two scenes ever written. A very changed version of them later appears in my non *Contrivance* short story, "What Happened Last Storm".

Justice is a secret revolutionary against Contrivance

in this draft, though she's conflicted as she volunteers at a community theater, working on putting on the musical *Annie,* staring all actual talented orphans. Thespian is her co director, a Deviser who volunteers on his off time. They bond unexpectedly, and Justice even subtly warns him of an upcoming attack, telling him to keep the Devisers away from that location the day of. Contrivance Headquarters is now set in NYC. Justice keeps some of her revolutionary friends from her original universe, but most of them are starting to fade in importance. I want her more entwined with the Devisers, but I'm not sure how.

Meanwhile, Malka pressures Lavender to adopt/apprentice one of the children from the show. Lavender likes the child, but doesn't feel ready to be something like a parent. (We'll come back to Lavender taking on an apprentice—with the tables turning a bit.)

The project didn't get terribly far. There was a lot of silliness here, though some important things start to crop up.

January 2017

I'm still in a rut on, "What is the plot of *Contrivance*?" For the first time in a long time, I start some new original fiction projects that actually get somewhere that aren't *Contrivance,* though *Contrivance* is still what mostly seems to play in my thoughts. I believe Malka's name started to change (to Malka) around here or a bit later.

My mental health is mostly improving, and I'm making plans to go to college.

October 2017

I've attempted to go to college in Boston, and things aren't going so well, and I'm in a psych ward.

I pretty much have my notebook for company, and I start trying out a new idea, combining *Contrivance* with one of the projects I started around January, which ends up looking a lot like the collaboration: traveling across universes. Even Justice finds a place as someone who had left the dark magical group and was now forced to return as part of the deal with the modern US government. I never actually *write* much of this, but the ideas were interesting in my head.

I leave Boston in early November and go home. Eight days later, I meet the love of my life.

April 2018

I moved in with my girlfriend in January, and I've even gone off meds. Everything is looking up, except for a set of mysterious physical health issues no one can diagnose. I barely write; I'm exploring a few new projects, but almost nothing goes on paper. I'm thinking I'll stop the weird experiments and try to get back to the core of what *Contrivance* is.

August 2018

Ah. So the house I moved into is full of toxic black mold, and I have a pre-existing respiratory condition. This gets remediated, though even more time passes as I fully recover. I stop going to NaNoWriMo events locally, though I still want to write for the challenge, despite a slow few months. I'm eager to start sorting ideas out again.

July 2019

Writing is still slow as I deal with lingering health issues. I got surgery in April for the respiratory issues. I recommend my dad (who I got the nose from) to my ENT. My ENT looks at my dad's general medical file and says, "I'm surprised you're not seeing ghosts."

My father abruptly dies at home a few weeks later.

But all I know is he's not answering his phone, and now my mom says mail is piling up in front of his obviously unopened front door. Grandma says he didn't put the trash bins down on trash pickup day. Something's not right.

I use my spare key to get into his house when he doesn't answer my knocks.

Yeah, something's not right: he's been dead for ten days.

August 2019

Coming back from a trip, a long car ride, I start trying to figure out some details for *Contrivance* again. I've figured out how to get Justice involved, as a former Deviser who left for the revolution and returned, much as she'd left the magicians in that one draft. Her primary Deviser relationship is not her friendship with Thespian (as it was in *Contrivance Chronicles;* Thespian appears much closer to another Deviser, Trace, here). Instead, Justice is focused on her romantic relationships with Rissa and Ritter (Rissa's husband), a possibility

I've imagined for a long time. Her age shifts slightly as needed. The revolution is becoming an important theme again.

I start to sort out Lavender and Francisco's relationship. While he pines, she just doesn't feel that way about anyone, but she's aware of his feelings, lending a strange edge to their otherwise close friendship. At least I'm not just throwing them at each other in the epilogue.

I've spent the last several months handling my father's estate amongst the new trauma. I'm busy, but I'm creating again.

November 2019

I finally have tenants move into Dad's house as a rental on the first of this month. Things are slowing down. I can work on other things now.

It's NaNo again, and I haven't finished it in four years at this point. But it's not like I sleep at night anymore, so I may as well write.

The first few days are slow. I go for miscellaneous *Contrivance* pieces, which is what I did the last time I finished. Some interesting ideas are coming out, but nothing of real substance.

My girlfriend, her friend/coworker, and I go to California on a business trip. In the car on the way there, I blare Evanescence through my headphones, stare out the window, and will myself to come up with something.

I'm exploring Malka and Lavender's relationship a lot again. It's… less hostile. It's still deeply screwed up for sure, but there's a norm of a superficial layer of civility at least, and there's obviously a lot of love somewhere in the messy mix.

So I try writing down ideas for things that could've happened in backstory.

One concept jumps out at me.

I do little but sit in the room and write the whole trip. My hands barely leave the keyboard. I don't sleep, I eat only something in the morning and then whatever I made for dinner for my girlfriend and her friend, and I'm distracted whenever I'm not writing.

This was when the practice interrogation was born.

It's a gripping idea. An especially dark take on the world the Devisers live in, the very real threat of a revolution. People out there want the Devisers hurt or dead. That's pretty much always been true, but more of an *emotional* factor than a logistic threat.

But in this draft, I say, *So what do they do about it?*

Of course, they have government security, all of those good things. But backstory for Lavender, at least, starts to include combat training and practicalities. I kind of skim over these things while I'm gripped by the interrogation idea, but I come back to the full depths of those later.

So I add into backstory that Malka prepared Lavender for a capture scenario. Gave her some data to keep a secret and spent sixty hours trying to get it out of her. In various eventual drafts, there was a little bit more preparation before this, or the idea that this was supposed to be more of the start, not the end, of this curriculum. In the end, it's a bit of both.

As I finish that up, along with a lot of the fallout, the next thing to explore is, of course, the payoff of this.

So I start a new document called "The Devisers Are Captured". Later, this becomes the opening scene of *Contrivance*. The Devisers are thrown into a hostage

situation, this time in Contrivance Headquarters as set
in Washington, DC. Offered the sadistic choice of picking
who will get interrogated for information first, Lavender
steps up. The others refuse to quietly agree, many
claiming they should go, and Lavender says they should
vote. Everyone votes for themselves, except for Malka,
who votes for Lavender.

Lavender quickly gets separated from the group while
the Devisers round on Malka for answers. Malka reveals
the practice. A book of emotional chaos ensues.

December 2019

Needing worldbuilding that adds up, I change what
Contrivance is again, this time opting to go back to the
Death Game genre origins I never truly escaped, an
annual televised simulation of a social collapse scenario,
participant households chosen at random, and one
surviving, while keeping it original fiction. I have an
awful cold a lot of the month, and so lie around and
write a lot. I sleep from about 10PM to 12AM, and 4AM to
10AM. In the middle, after the nightmares, I write.

February 2020

Just starting to see the PTSD calm down for a bit, I
keep rolling with my current *Contrivance* train of ideas.
Eventually, I run into a wild take on the fallout of their
capture, which is, *What if they did the practice again?*

But it's different this time. Lavender, paranoid that,
while their capture and rescue did not result in any
leaked information, it would be easy to get information
out of her in the future if only their captors tried to play

the Devisers against each other, hurting someone she loved and asking her the questions, asks Malka for a new curriculum: resisting the other Devisers being in pain, though without letting any of them know this is happening. They're still furious over finding out about the original practice, and none of them would agree to help. Besides, Lavender doesn't want to expose them to it.

Lavender definitely is more than just a victim here, a direction she's been heading in for a while, much more of an active participant and instigator in the questionable activities her and Malka engage in.

All kinds of subplots come out of this, and of course, the question: how does this one pay off?

May 2020

There's a pandemic. The world seems to be ending. Talk about my novel now being timely. My grandmother passes shortly after the beginning of quarantine. I get engaged.

Meanwhile, I start posting *Contrivance* pieces on a website of my own, snippets that are out of order, presented as a bit of a puzzle. A lot of it doesn't go neatly together yet.

July 2020

My mental health declines. The PTSD at the one year anniversary. Grandma's death. The psychosis. I go back on meds, though I stop attending therapy (now on Zoom) a few months later as I improve. I'm still working on multiple projects and producing a lot of words, mostly focused on the *I'll Give You* series as a break.

December 2020

My wife and I got married last month. I'm doing well, really. I published my first book, a non *Contrivance* "side project" that got out of hand and is now a popular series of its own. I've taken down the *Contrivance* website and start to post *Contrivance* online chapter by chapter as I did the other project, now officially starting for basically the first time since the fan fiction universe somewhere other than Lavender's job interview: with "The Devisers Are Captured". This ages Lavender up a little. I try to make it mostly linear, sensical for new readers, and kill my darlings a bit. Here we go.

I also post the first companion, "How Justice and Rissa Fell in Love Again", because there's too much content for it not to.

February 2021

I publish my second book, still not *Contrivance*. That "side project" really got out of hand. I've started teaching webinars, I've started going to butler school. There's a lot going on.

Still, I love the Devisers. Focusing on them more again feels like coming home to old friends. Friends you've known too well, too long to think they're perfect, but that feel easy, like home anyway.

May 2021

I take a little staycation, a few day writing retreat alone at a nearby hotel, using rewards points that we got to keep through the pandemic. It doesn't go well. I don't take care of myself, lost in my words, around Chapter 9 of Contrivance, and my mental state spirals, and I self harm for the first time in many years, the first since Boston. My wife takes me home early.

July 2021

I'm now running a local alternative sexuality group, and I publish *Service Slave Secrets (Volume One)*, the first years of my blog on the subject, to a nice reception. The *I'll Give You* series flows.

I try going off my meds briefly, gradually cutting down with the thought that I'll stop when it starts to affect my sleep, as that's the easiest way to measure the minimum dosage. However, my sleep doesn't really suffer, but I abruptly realize, five minutes overdue for the first dose I've totally skipped, that I've been absolutely miserable, and can't hear my own thoughts over the music hallucinations I mistook for a song stuck in my head, among others. I go back to the full dosage that night.

We go on our first vacation since before the pandemic, and I get road trip time to think.

There are still some details about the ending of *Contrivance* this time around that I'm figuring out. I need it to be… relevant. But it's coming together.

Soon, I post another companion focusing on the other Devisers (not Lavender or Malka), "Francisco's Guide to Insomnia."

November 2021

NaNoWriMo isn't going so well, but I publish

Book Two of the main *I'll Give You* trilogy and post
a *Contrivance* backstory companion, "We Are All That We
Have Lost".

Several months into the "health kick" that's taken an
especially dark spiral recently—purging and fasting and
overexercising—I accept that I have an eating disorder—
all of the symptoms of anorexia, not quite underweight
—and start the cycle of *on again off again* commitment to
recovery. I don't need to weight restore, but this cycle has
got to stop. I start to talk about it with the people close to
me.

March 2022

Oh my God. It's done.

Just as suddenly as it sounds, I publish *Contrivance*, in
the same week as *The Second IGY Companion.*

It's surreal. Finishing any of my books was surreal, but
this one especially.

It's certainly an interesting month. I'm still bouncing
back and forth on the eating habits, now with my wife's
help supervising three meals a day for a while, starting to
sort out my disordered thoughts around food, focusing
on the fact that skinny seems to represent *productive* for
me, and that I'm actually more productive—like
publishing two books in a week, productive—if I just suck
it up and eat. I'm also finally learning how to drive.

I keep my heart open to more of *Contrivance*, but for
now, I think I might actually be done.

August 2022

I can't help myself. There's a sequel.

But I love what's coming in Book Two. I love the addition to the main cast who actually works, I love that this isn't a plotline I've done to death before, I love that it feels true to the *sentiment* of Contrivance.

All right. One more book.

In the last few months, I've also started donating plasma, started a Little Free Library, have been working on my newest blog, A Productive Hannah, and published *Service Slave Secrets: Volume Two*.

August is a hard month for me, though. I'd like to blame it on hormonal, non psychiatric med changes, but I'm not sure. Right on the heels of some major anniversaries involving my father's birth and death, symptoms, especially the eating issues, flare, and burnout threatens.

I spend a week on vacation in Boston, and vow to take September off from events.

October 2022

I post another companion story as well, a Justice centric piece that's been in my head for a long time.

Book Two is flowing. A lot of it in my head, some of it on paper, and a second chapter actually gets posted.

I'm back to events, but we've gotten into camping, a welcome reprieve from most of the world. I'm trying to find balance, and overall, my events and writings are going really well. I'm trying to clear my plate a little, to publish *The Schizophrenia Diaries*, to be able to focus on fiction more.

We'll see what the future holds.

I WENT OFF MY MEDICATION AND HALLUCINATED EVANESCENCE

What it says on the tin.

And it was, honestly, probably the most emo thing to ever happen to me.

Let me back up and elaborate.

I didn't impulsively and abruptly go off the med (though the occasional *flush all of it!* urge is strong). What happened was this:

When I started Seroquel about a year ago (the only psychiatric med I've been on in years), I was prescribed 100mg, one pill at night. It worked like a charm for several months, but then I started getting the token grogginess in the mornings. At the advice of my psychiatrist, I went down to 75mg. Except that they don't make Seroquel in 75mg tablets, so I actually took three 25mg pills at night. Okay, so that was fine. Grogginess gone, but sleep was still good, along with mood, psychosis, etc. I was told that if need be, I could go back up to 100mg and give her a call for a new prescription.

During a week about two months ago where I was having trouble sleeping due to other factors, I went back up to 100mg, taking four of the 25mg pills. I kind of meant to go back down after that week or so, but the 100mg was working well and the grogginess hadn't returned, so I stayed, and was given a new prescription to go back to 100mg.

Now, I was back to the one, 100mg pill, again free to go down if it was too much. This pill still seemed to hit me differently than the four 25mg ones, and I felt the grogginess return. I wasn't sure if this was again other factors or the meds, so I tried cutting the 100mg (half, then cutting one of those halves in half again) and taking 75mg. (Bear with me through the numbers for a minute.)

I did eventually attribute the extra grogginess to probably external factors, but I also didn't feel any worse for taking the 75mg, and my psychiatrist had emphasized again and again taking the lowest effective dose, especially since you can develop a tolerance to Seroquel over time. So I took the 75mg for a few weeks. I felt stressed a lot, but attributed it to having a lot to do. I was still writing like crazy, and mostly keeping up.

Then I got curious, and went down to just taking the half (50mg). I again noticed no difference. In hindsight, my mood, focus, and energy had really begun to drop, but nothing crazy. There was no difference in my sleep. I fell asleep promptly enough, slept relatively soundly, dreamt (for better or worse), and woke with as much ease as ever. Now, I'd never been on only 50mg before and I didn't, at the time, notice a difference.

Thinking that odd, I kept going and went down to 25mg (a quarter of the pill, being all out of the former prescription). I did that for a few days and felt terrible but didn't attribute it to the meds. I was depressed and irritable as hell, but had attributed this to another problem. (I did have… something during that time frame I'm still not sure of. Stomach flu? My wife got a version too, whatever it was. That definitely wasn't the med's fault, but it was a separate set of symptoms.) I again didn't notice anything different in my sleep, the thing I felt so sure I was going to notice a change in if the meds were doing anything useful. When I went on the Seroquel at first, it was the sleep I noticed instantly. I still had some energy, and although I thought it was too hot for my usual walks most of the time, I still enjoyed long swings on the swingset in the yard, this week to the soundtrack of a newly discovered old song by Evanescence I was really enjoying.

Finally, I said, *To hell with it*, and one night skipped the med altogether. And I lay there. And lay there. Sleep wasn't coming. Even sleepiness wasn't coming. I was irritable, depressed, mildly panicked, and incredibly restless. My head was pounding to the beat of that Evanescence song and it was stuck in my head playing on full blast, drowning out other thoughts. Sensory overload coming from inside my brain. But it felt mostly just like having a song really stuck in my head, which for me I know always works a little more like hallucination than it does for other people. (You ever tried describing having a song stuck in your head to a hypothetical someone who has no idea what that means? Now there's a thought exercise about sanity.)

But I realized *something* was up, caved, and took the full 100mg, the last dose that I knew I had felt good on, and had only started going down from because of grogginess I now attributed to something else. Within fifteen minutes or so, I was calm, half asleep, and the volume of the Evanescence song had gone from 99 to 5. It was like someone just *whoop* turned the volume dial down in my brain. Still there, all the same qualities, but at about five percent of the volume. I could hear other thoughts.

Oh. So that explained a lot.

So, I'm back at 100mg. I'm open to going back down to 75mg depending on if the grogginess seems to return, and if my mood changes if I do go back to 75mg. But for now, back at square one.

I think it was a worthwhile experiment even if it didn't go super well—and even if it took me a while to realize it hadn't gone super well. No tragic consequences; it wasn't really done recklessly, and I do believe in finding the lowest effective dose and not mindlessly settling on the current med regimen, even if it's just proving where you're already at; it also gave me some more confidence in *the meds do important things* for when I get those med flushing urges. Today, I'm thinking, *God bless Seroquel,* but I'm sure that urge will come back at some point.

Besides, *I went off my medication and hallucinated Evanescence* should really earn me my official Emo Kid Card. Rock on.

THIS IS WHAT SCHIZOPHRENIA FEELS LIKE

This is what schizophrenia feels like,
　It's hearing a crowded coffee shop in a silent office, and hearing nothing in a crowded coffee shop
　It's a fake flash of light here, a fake bit of white noise there
　It's an object looking upside down, wider, shorter, three inches to the left, and back again, and back again
　It's turning down the music and realizing half the volume's in my head
　It's a phone, doorbell, alarm that rings for three days
　It's hearing my name whispered from the next bathroom stall
　It's something always in my peripheral vision that's never really there
　It's the "dog" that never needs feeding but can trip me on the stairs
　It's the "corpse" that I can't shake in the empty spot in the bed
　It's the "demons" that dance in impossible lines
　It's real shadows taking shapes and shadows coming

from no real object
It's putting on noise cancelling headphones that can't
cancel what's in my head; *oh*
This is what schizophrenia feels like,
It's *real* and it's *not real.*
This is what schizophrenia feels like,
It's the, "*Even* schizophrenia doesn't make you
unworthy of love," like I thought it was the exception
It's the caricature of a shouting schizophrenic racist
like that's all we are
It's the, "Cat? I don't see a cat," even when you know it
breaks my mind
It's the romantic tragedy trope for no reason because it
sounds extreme
It's the, "I'm not qualified to help you," from someone
with a wall of degrees and a fake smile
It's the *no, I wouldn't cure myself if I could—*
It's the *no, I don't know if I'm hallucinating—*
It's the *no, I can't explain—*
It's the, "Did you take your meds today?"
It's the playing pretend at first, then
It's the uncomfortable expression; when you started
talking mental health, you expected depression or
anxiety; why?
This is what schizophrenia feels like,
It's *too much* and it's *not enough.*
This is what schizophrenia feels like,
It's *the pharmacy isn't real and neither are you*
It's *I have to protect my telepathic notebook*
It's *I have to flush the meds flush the meds FLUSH THE
MEDS—*
It's *you want to hurt me* and it's, *Let go of me—!*
It's *I have to run away*

It's *but only the house is safe*
It's *I don't even know anymore*
This is what schizophrenia feels like,
It's *true* and it's *not true.*
This is what schizophrenia feels like,
It's staring at the wall seeing nothing
It's staring at the wall seeing everything you can't
It's sinking into a daydream the way I'd sink to the
bottom of the ocean
It's *the deeper I sink, the harder it is to surface*
It's *but sometimes it's beautiful down here*
It's characters three steps ahead of my mind
It's *the whole room doesn't go away for you?*
It's not noticing fingers snapped in front of my face
It's limbs going limp
It's *you're supposed to be able to control waking dreams?*
It's *how do I get back?*
It's *no I don't control who my characters are*
This is what schizophrenia feels like,
It's *story* and it's *fact.*
This is what schizophrenia feels like,
It's a poem I'll never get right.

ON DEVELOPING PTSD… AFTER WRITING CHARACTERS WITH PTSD, AS A SCHIZOPHRENIC

There are a lot of complaints about how writers (and other creators) portray mental health, and perhaps one of the most mentioned issues is PTSD.

I've been writing characters with PTSD for about a decade. But I didn't have PTSD of my own until just a few years ago.

Looking back over old works—while there are things I would do differently just because I've grown as a writer —I don't find my portrayals of PTSD that inaccurate. My research was thorough, including the personal experiences of others. The insertion of fictionalized personal anecdotes of symptoms and some of the emotional charge, as in the after the fact pieces, is missing. But I don't feel dissatisfied with a lot of it.

Shortly after the incident that gave me the PTSD, it took one pointed question from my therapist for me to literally say, "Yes, I've also read the PTSD diagnostic criteria." I knew my stuff, and even while still standing there with my father's ten day old corpse, I was very aware that it was the kind of thing that tends to leave you with long term effects. The question from my therapist came only a few weeks later, not long enough for a formal diagnosis—something else I knew from research—but I could see the road I was on.

The new symptoms felt strangely familiar. Hypervigilance was something I'd read about, wrote about, for so many years, that it didn't *feel* new, especially as someone with pre existing sensory issues and anxiety. It was so tightly woven into characters' lives that finding it in my own felt kind of like a fan of any work stepping into that world. Of course you've never gone to Hogwarts, *Harry Potter* fans, but you'd kind of know your way around, wouldn't you?

I did find it interesting that I developed the hypervigilance, since it would've done me no good in the traumatic incident. Nightmares, too, beyond what I'd developed as an anxious child with an overactive imagination, felt strangely… familiar. I'd spent enough restless nights writing about characters waking up in a cold sweat that waking up like that myself before turning to the notebook or laptop didn't feel so new. Flashbacks, too.

But what really made trauma feel so familiar? Was it really just so many years of inflicting it on characters? Was it pre existing anxiety?

But here was another complication, a major

wrench to throw in any comorbid disorder group: the schizophrenia.

Over time, my flashbacks manifested a significant portion of the time as true hallucination, something that I was used to from schizophrenia. Now, here's an almost funny thing: in fiction, one of the most critiqued techniques of portraying PTSD flashbacks and nightmares is in the vivid, clear, straightforward nature. Real PTSD can give you a flashback to one sense but not another, to something somehow connected to the trauma but not directly, show you a hazy overlay, or be an almost purely emotional rather than sensory response. Nightmares often mix up elements of trauma with random elements from your life, not just playing the trauma again and again.

But that's hard to portray in fiction, especially in visual media like movies, and especially when flashbacks and dreams are also used as narrative devices. Hence, you get those straightforward, easy to comprehend for the audience cutaway scenes.

But for me, schizophrenia mixing with PTSD *did* make daytime flashbacks manifest as clear cut hallucinations. There wasn't just the sensory confusion or disconnected emotional responses; I'd be looking at/hallucinating my father's corpse in the corner of the room, or in the bed—which became one of my biggest triggers—or perpetually behind me. The laughably oversimplified PTSD portrayal was, oddly, spot on for me much of the time.

Now, I have to remember that in all cases, my PTSD is not my characters' PTSD, and none of them have comorbid schizophrenia. But one reason trauma felt so familiar to me was that it was already a part of the characters already living in my head. And all of the research involved in making that feel real. Another, that the schizophrenia induced hallucinations and anxiety I'd already lived with went a lot like the way PTSD flashbacks eventually manifested for me. Perhaps the biggest complicating factor: my much thinner line between reality and fiction than most peoples'—if my characters experienced anything, it was much more like *I* was experiencing it than even most creative types would agree with—so maybe, in a way, I'd had a bit of self created trauma and PTSD all along. Or maybe it was just tortured artist syndrome.

But again, I risk the horrifically oversimplified portrayal of PTSD trope in fiction even if I'm true to some of my experiences, because of what schizophrenia makes it like, an interesting conundrum, and without characters with comorbid schizophrenia, it remains inaccurate.

After my traumatic incident, I wrote a lot of dark material for an already dark project, mostly in the middle phase of largely sleepless nights. I was especially unpacking a pre existing character's trauma from both previous and new drafts, especially in the immediate fallout, a time period I'd seemed to drift away from before, with many characters' primary traumas existing far into backstory, aggravated by a dark world. Was it my own recent trauma that drew me into that time period, or was it simply time for it anyway? Hard to tell. Likely at least a bit of both.

Though, wallowing in horror, gore, and otherwise macabre genres is a common trauma trope in itself, something like self inflicted exposure therapy—though I stayed away from my exact triggers, decomposition and the like. But I'd almost always had that draw to dark fiction, pre trauma—again, why? My pre trauma mental health symptoms—schizophrenia, anxiety—did seem to draw me more deeply into those, much like PTSD symptoms do for many others. It's almost like my mental health experience was always *so close* to PTSD, but with no real cause, a crucial part of it, before it developed. Some comorbidities are already more likely than others, too; maybe I was always all but doomed to develop PTSD at the slightest provocation, and I got a bit more than *the slightest.*

Things I think about. Plenty to unpack for myself and characters both.

PSYCHOSIS AND BEYOND AS SELF SOOTHING

Farrah, my recurring puppy hallucination, often appears when I'm in distress.

While I don't qualify as something like schizoaffective, which is different anyway, the state of my emotions and the state of my psychosis usually line up in some way. Negative moods lead to more obvious psychotic symptoms than positive ones.

If Farrah appears without me being in distress, I frequently wonder if, subconsciously, I am. Sometimes the answer was yes all along. Sometimes I'm now so worried about finding the (perhaps nonexistent) source of the problem, or about the psychosis itself, that, in any case, I'm upset now. Sometimes, I accept the hallucination as random.

Still, I have often wondered, *Why Farrah?* She is my only specific recurring hallucination that I don't understand the source of. The ones that are basically PTSD flashbacks gone wild—make sense. But why the dog?

Recently, feeling stressed and with no such

appearance from Farrah, I realized that I kind of missed her, would have liked her there. Even if we want to label all psychosis as bad, she's a free, ethical forever puppy that can't really eat or poop, and who doesn't want that?

I wondered if Farrah was a psychotic/automatic self soothing technique. I can't control it, but maybe some dysfunctional chemicals somewhere in my brain are saying, "Hey; calm down. Here's a puppy." Or, *Here's some free dopamine.*

I'd much rather the dog than the ringing phone that I heard most of that day, at least.

I had to think about other psychotic symptoms as forms of self soothing.

Dissociation is not usually defined as psychosis by itself, but I feel like it's a key part of my psychosis experience, so to speak. My early psychotic episodes frequently involved dissociation that manifested as akinetic catatonia. Dissociation very commonly has origins in maladapted self soothing, mentally separating yourself from an upsetting or traumatic situation. Dissociative Identity Disorder (formerly Multiple Personality Disorder) especially frequently has roots in traumatic stress early in life.

Dissociating was something I did frequently before I showed definitive signs of psychosis, mostly in the form of intense daydreams. Maladaptive daydreaming is also not technically seen as a form of psychosis (and is not widely recognized) due to the separation that remains between fantasy and reality—but my lines there *do* get very blurry due to other psychosis symptoms.

In any case, these daydreams take over my head somewhat beyond my control when something in me wants to escape. They're certainly addictive and can be a disabling distraction, but also feel crucial for me as a fiction writer who escapes to my stories' worlds.

One of the first symptoms my parents reported to mental health professionals was my tendency to spend multiple hours per day swinging on the swingset in our backyard, listening to a song on repeat with headphones, totally spaced out. Daydreaming. How upset I got when this was not possible for one reason or another. This has followed me throughout my life.

Even last summer, before my wife and I got a swingset in our new backyard, I walked to the park and back daily, sometimes multiple trips per day, to spend hours on the swings, with a song on repeat and my daydreams. It was about a mile walk each way and the temperature regularly approached 120*F. I was not deterred.

Some daydreams, the type I have on my office floor in dissociative states, tend to be cathartic wallowing on a character's behalf. They don't echo the situation I'm upset about exactly, but branch out from the specific core feeling I'm having. They won't echo just *sad* nor exactly *there is a pandemic and I can't see my friends*, but maybe *lonely.* Sometimes these daydreams allow me to cry or fully experience emotions that I hadn't been able to release or wallow in initially.

I experience other types of dissociation, too. Some distressing. But frequently, there's the blank dissociation where my mind seems to go nowhere or into the void or however one might phrase it. This might be the *anywhere is better than here* dissociation, where the daydreams are not coming (yet, anymore, or period) but I'm sure not ready to go back to reality.

Other symptoms—delusion. Now, delusion in the colloquial sense is very often a form of self soothing, especially in the form of denial, which is also a stage of grief. But some delusions are distressing, especially the paranoid kind, and while that is true for me, others can, in a backwards way, be comforting.

Reality breaks for me easily. The feeling some people get from watching things like *The Matrix* or *Inception,* times ten, is easy to induce in me. And when it happens, my brain needs an explanation, fast. There is no time for logic—that something was fiction, a joke, a lie, a coincidence—and so my brain grasps at straws to explain the thing away. While false and sometimes overly convoluted, the delusion fills that need—creating a "logical" if sometimes distressing reality—until the real world can set back in.

Psychosis and other symptom sets are often not *just* a dysfunctional coping mechanism—and some of these automatic self soothing techniques only attempt to solve the problem another symptom created. But it's still interesting to look at some incidents of symptoms in that light.

IMAGES YOU CAN'T SHAKE

I'm in a dream. There was a beginning, but now I'm rapidly pacing through the private school I attended so many years ago, turning the corner at the landing like it was yesterday. But this portion of the hallway isn't quite right—there are doors, doors, doors, on one side, and I'm throwing them open as I go, getting flashes of what's in the room. I know I'm looking for something, but I'm not sure what. Each room seems to get me closer. They become more and more disorderly, and more and more frequently feature a bed. Then a few things happen almost all at once:

I realize I'm dreaming.

I realize what's behind the last door.

I throw open the last door before I can stop myself anyway.

Dad, of course, dead for ten days, of course, in the dream and filling my vision as I bolt upright, gasping, a scream diffusing in my throat.

And, I'm pretty sure lastly, my morning alarm goes off.

So, morning. I sleepily breeze through my morning checklists. Wash up, same clothes as always. One mile walk. Wave to the same group of retirees and dogs as usual. An hour of notebook drafting, my writing ritual right now. My daily housewife routine. Brunch, toast as almost always, at 9:30. Create stability where you can, y'know. And my autism loves routine.

Still, my mind finds time to come back to the dream, writing about it, pondering sources—a visit at my mom's house yesterday, rife with family pictures of those long gone, or maybe a recent pre Halloween *Goosebumps* story rewatch that featured decay —and putting on one of my favorite songs for *one of those days*, and generally wallowing.

Nothing dramatic, but feeling, over two years later, still desperate to shake the one image I can't get rid of, nightmare, flashback, hallucination, or otherwise. One of my characters said in a recent chapter, of her own trauma, "*Of course I have to do it again. I do it again when I close my eyes. (…) I do it again when I zone out too hard. Don't you get that?*"

I get that.

I knew when I found my father that I wasn't going to be able to shake that image. It's not really one of those visuals that you process in the moment. It's one of those… *we'll need to keep coming back to this,* do it again, and again, to process.

I felt very calm in the moment in a way (returning to the car where my now-wife was waiting, she thought all was well based on my body language)—and very determined that no one *else* see that image who didn't have to, swearing to myself as I walked back down my father's stairs, *professionals only,* and very aware that I'd decided to get here before my mother's planned check in later—perhaps dissociated, but despite my day to day anxiety, I've always been strangely good in an emergency —and also very aware that it was all going to hit me later.

I just kind of figured, *I'll have PTSD now.* That was a trauma angle I hadn't really thought of before, researching and writing it in fiction: the awareness at the point of the trauma of the future effects. I still don't think I processed it fully for some time.

Now, I'm working on a backstory companion piece in which someone asks the same character mentioned above, very shortly post trauma, what it is she's feeling.

She responds that while she's not sure, it feels like *grief* (though no one has died), and when asked for what, she says, *For* before.

I know I felt grief both for my father's actual death and for *before*. Before the trauma, before the PTSD, before the nightmares, the extra hypervigilance, the flashbacks, the ones that became hallucinations. For *before* that image. I grieved my father, but also something I had never defined enough to know I could lose.

It wasn't any traditional *loss of innocence* grief story, and I don't really think of it that way—I was still an adult with an awareness of the world at the time, though I think I aged a lot in the months after, not only trauma but adulting logistics (probate court and beyond), the independence to pursue my own projects, whatnot—but some people certainly might see it that way.

Maybe it's masochistic, but in a way—simply as a longtime writer of trauma and PTSD and images characters can't shake, and as a person who questioned my own resilience—I'm almost grateful for the experience.

Maybe that's screwed up, but it's at least a better

emotion than *only* sitting around going *woe is me,* and I certainly wouldn't wish the experience on my mother or anyone else who might, in some parallel universe, have walked into the house that day, or, I guess, in the ten days before it. The house was up for sale. I'm not sure if the realtor had access to the house without being in touch with my father—we were, strangely, ultimately not in contact long—but some home buyers to be may have seriously dodged a bullet. And if my father had to die, then I can only suppose it was all the same post mortem to him, and it appeared he passed in his sleep, at home, which many people would consider—if you must die one way or another—basically ideal.

I always wanted to do research via experience where I could, or utilize past experiences as research for fiction. I made trips to the archery range to try it out back when I was writing *Hunger Games* fan fiction; more recently, I responded to a reader's comment of appreciation on a requested companion to one of my original fiction series: ~~Someone should, I bought a damn shock collar to research this scene and yes it was set to 99.~~ *Thank you!* (To be amply clear, this was an alternative sexuality erotica piece and the product was safely tested on myself in that context, not an animal.)

And I've thought about doing more *out there* things in the name of research—if there's value in recreating my characters' specific traumas/if it could be safely done myself. Things like that.

So sometimes I feel like I'm experiencing my real trauma through the lens of writing, research. There are novelty tees and mugs out there with a message like, *Warning: I'm a writer. Anything you say or do may be used in a story.* And that goes for me, too. A distressing

symptom can still have me running for a pen.
   Or a blog post.

JUST ANOTHER DAY, MAYBE

It's been a long day. Hard to say why.

Part of me wants to say it's just physical health stuff, and I can't tell if that's strangely logical or minimizing my own feelings. It could be that my best friend, more like family, left for a job in another state today. It could just be a long day.

I feel like I was unfocused a lot of this morning, though I also got some important things done, scheduling classes I'll be teaching in the new year, and even almost winning a game of ping pong with my wife (getting close is an accomplishment for me and most people).

But by late afternoon, I was wallowing in angsty daydreams. Making dinner went like this: put water on to boil. Set timer. Sit on couch, dissociate into my characters' distress. Timer goes off. Stumble over and add pasta. Set timer. Sit on couch, return to daydream. Stare, sniffle a little. Timer goes off. Stir pasta, mind still half somewhere else. Set timer. Sit on couch—

By the time I got dinner on the table, I was on the edge of tears. Over… nothing in particular, or maybe things that happened to my characters that were not even quite canonical in *their* universes, dramatized montages, and certainly fictional in ours. My wife prodded at it—asking about both of the potential reasons for a long day I started with—but I shrugged it off, wasn't up for much conversation, and mostly wanted to be left alone to fully return to my other worlds. I asked about her day instead.

Finishing up dinner, unable to control the tears, I sat on the floor in the bathroom with the door closed and let them fall. It's hard to explain the kind of tears you don't really want to be soothed out of, especially when you're not sure they're over anything in particular, whether real or fictional. It's like reading a sad book, or watching a sad movie, that is sad, yes, but good, so you don't want to be interrupted. But not like, the tragic ending, or an especially climactic character death. More like one of those sad establishing character montages, like the exposition behind *Do You Want To Build a Snowman,* or the notorious, silent first minutes of *Up.*

But in any case, I wasn't ready to be done wallowing, so I hid for a few minutes until they came back under control, and my wife had gone upstairs.

Then I went and did the dishes and cleaned up the kitchen, did some other evening tasks, before retreating to my office, door shut, which isn't super frequent and is usually for focus (really, to keep the cats out and not on top of my notebook or keyboard). And wallowed on the floor again.

To complete the wallowing, I heard the vaguely sad piano music. This wasn't so surprising, for a second, as in place of my usual rain sounds or *Harry Potter* themed ASMR, I've been using a calm piano Spotify playlist as my office background noise the last few days. Except I was ninety-nine percent sure that my phone wasn't playing anything—I had just brought it up from downstairs with me, where I'd shut the music while using the phone as a timer. But there was the piano, clear, but soft, barely rising above the hum of the air conditioner. Not any tune I recognized, nor anything coherent. It would pause, then pick up with a different key or melody or volume, or I would just hear a random isolated note here or there for a minute. Finally, I threw myself up off the floor and checked the phone. Nothing. Not coming from the phone. Just me.

This struck me as interesting. Previously, I wrote about going down on my medication and hallucinating the Evanescence song I'd had on repeat. I was—back on my regular med regimen—again hallucinating music, but it was a hodgepodge of the (sixteen hour) instrumental playlist I'd had on shuffle. I'd wondered before if I'd done something wrong with the Evanescence besides the med changes. If perhaps something in it emotionally was a trigger (some of the chorus lyrics included *can you hear me, can you hear me,* which was almost begging to be hallucinated), or if I just really needed to lay off the repeat button. But here I was again.

Back on the floor, pondering that, finally distracted properly from the daydreams, I also noticed something else. I don't remember where it began now—just a few hours later—but I had the thought, *I'm still at the Marriott,* and it was becoming more and more gripping.

So, as context, in May, I used some of the extra Marriott rewards points my wife and I had sitting around from pre pandemic business travel, and had my own writer's retreat/staycation at a nearby hotel. It was supposed to be three nights. I—and my wife—had anticipated that things might get *a little weird.* That I would stay up a bit late, have a snack instead of dinner, and get super absorbed in my fictional worlds, using the retreat to block out distracting reality for a few days. But things got *a lot weird.*

I think because I underestimated the physical neglect. On my last full day, I realized I hadn't brought any water, and had only had a mouthful of tap water to take my meds, and milk, since I arrived. I remedied this with a bottle of water and a Gatorade from the sundry store, but I mostly forgot about them after a few sips of each. I had neglected real food almost entirely, despite the fact I had taught a *class* about cooking on the road. When I did the pre pandemic business travel with my wife, I made us nice crock pot meals and simple side dishes in a hotel room with nothing more than an old microwave and leaking mini fridge. At home, I eat at least two scheduled meals a day with her. Yet, alone and lost in writing, I had stuck mostly to toast, fruit, cereal, and dessert. I also acquired a microwaveable mac and cheese cup as something closer to real food, but I later found it mysteriously still sitting in the microwave, filled with water to the right line, but uncooked and abandoned.

I had stayed up almost all night the first night, despite my usual at home bedtime before ten o'clock, then dragged myself downstairs early to check out the continental breakfast. My sleep was weird the next night, too. By that last full day, I uncharacteristically impulsively took a caffeine pill (100mg) midday as someone sensitive to caffeine. I had, realizing how late I'd stayed up and that I didn't want to be in a coma all day, not taken the full dose of my antipsychotic med at least one night, either.

I became a total wreck, and failing to find anything better available, had started self harming with manicure scissors, for the first time in almost four years. I calmed down enough to throw on some antibiotic ointment and call my wife and tell her all this. She was calm, appropriately concerned but understanding, and asked if I wanted to come home. I wasn't sure. I tried to write some more. But by midnight, I realized the words had stopped coming that morning. After another phone call, she picked me up and took me home.

Anyway, you can see how this makes sense as a source of a delusion. There's a lot of stuff already wrapped up in there. Lying on my office floor tonight, I felt myself sinking into the idea that I had never left that Marriott. That everything after was a hallucination, a dream, a… I wasn't sure what.

But we went to Tahoe, I thought, over and over, trying to counter the issue with more travel. In July, we took a trip with a friend and my Mom (a delayed Mother's Day present for the busy schoolteacher) up to Lake Tahoe, got a beautiful Airbnb with gorgeous views and regular meals and sleep and meds. (Yet, it's a picture of the Strip I took from my twenty-third floor Marriott room that lives on as my desktop background; I spent almost the whole time in front of that window, watching over the top of my notebook the flashing lights, the monorail passing by, the High Roller going around. The crazy city I've always called home.) It was like the *never left the Marriott* theory had come in a flash of enlightenment, but I was still thinking my way through it. But… Tahoe. And everything else.

I also had a slight grip, in a way, on the fact that the *never left the Marriott* thing was the actual delusion, and I was trying to avoid sinking into it, but also desperately mentally countering it, as if it *needed* to be countered and not ignored. I felt a phantom burning in my wrists that is usually a *you want to cut* kind of physical manifestation, but I thought, *Or I'm dreaming.* And they would hurt in real life because of what I had done with the manicure scissors that afternoon.

And then, strangely, lying on my office floor, it all kind of went away. The daydreams were a vague temptation, but had no strong, magnetic grip on me. The piano notes grew further and further apart, then quieted, and there was just the neighbors talking in their yard on the other side of the wall. The Marriott theory was like something I'd read in a book once—interesting, but not demanding. The phantom burning subsided as I eyed the long healed, faint marks.

I took a swingset break, made us a light dessert and tried not to think about the calories, cleaned the kitchen again, checked the Internet, started writing this—the most I've written all day—and got ready for bed.

Well, let this weird day be over, then, and we'll see what tomorrow looks like.

WOULD I CURE MYSELF?

After the whole finding my father's ten day old corpse thing, I didn't really sleep for about a year, until I went back on meds.

I think that this was understandable. I think there are just some things it's more dysfunctional to *not* be screwed up by for an extended period of time than it is to be super resilient about, and that's just one of them.

I don't know what would've happened if I'd gone back on meds sooner. I put it off, not wanting to hop right back on chemicals when, for some amount of time, I was, simply, just going to be screwed up for a while. After about a year, though, I decided it was time. The level of functionality I wanted then, compared to what I'd wanted before, was just not going to be achieved without meds.

In any case, the year of questionable sleep.

At the time, I'd been prone to going to bed around nine or ten, staying up a few more hours on my computer or with a book or my notebook, then sleeping in until ten or eleven. (Now, I'm more of a morning person, with firmer schedules.) But post trauma, after going to sleep as normal, I'd wake up around one and be up until after four or five.

I used this middle of the night time almost exclusively to write. Or, I might message with my best friend, who was working some late shifts at the time, mostly *about* writing. It wasn't a time for house sorting, no lease drafting, no exhibits, no affidavits, no legal notices.

Despite the constant exhaustion, I often find myself looking back on this time period strangely fondly. I was in a creative peak. I was making constant breakthroughs on a plot I'd been stuck on for years, and churning out huge amounts of words, but what I really remember was my suddenly infinite amount of *emotional* writing energy.

I could write all the angst and fear and pain in the world, drawing from a seemingly bottomless well of inspiration, without emotional burnout. I didn't *tire* of writing emotion, didn't start staring at the page blankly after too many hours of creating deeply emotional content rife with tragedy. I was *living* buried so deeply in real trauma that fiction seemed infinitely cathartic, not burning through my usual well of emotions and then needing to be put down for a while.

I spent the year or so mostly *creating*, but towards the one year mark, when I went back on meds, I also started posting fiction regularly online for the first time in a long time (and that had been mostly fan fiction; now, it was original work). I went back to writing mostly linearly and still prolifically, went back to doing more editing, formatting, advertising, all of those bits, the things that come with an Internet presence.

Right around the one year mark, I started this blog. I think it was around when I started to see the light of seeking more treatment that I realized I had so much real darkness to talk about.

After the one year mark, I started self publishing books, started teaching webinars, running a social group, going to butler school, and more. Left therapy, kept the meds.

Still, so much of what I've accomplished since that one year mark—the things that sound good on paper: posting, publication, teaching, earning income, the plaudits—was, creatively speaking, born of that sleepless, nightmare and flashback and hallucination and dissociation ridden year. Of course, the pandemic happened in the middle, too, along with my grandmother's death, and other things to keep stocking that dark creative well.

Meds, aided by time, gave me the mind to be outwardly productive, but it was that year just post trauma, still off meds, that truly offered the creative side.

Of course, I'm still creating. But sometimes it's not the same. Before I adjusted to the meds, there was a brief time my daydreams weren't as vivid, and I feared that. Considered going down a bit. There are a lot of times I wish Farrah, my puppy recurring hallucination, "appeared" to me more often, like a weird form of company. Even the nightmares and flashbacks, while unpleasant in the moment, stock something creative in my brain it's hard to pin down and I wouldn't want to do totally without.

I honestly don't aim for *symptom free*. I think psychosis and the rest of my mental health is a part of who I am to be balanced but not eliminated, just like any other. Imagine if someone offered you a magic pill to never feel, say, mildly depressed again. Would you take it? It's likely you don't want to be cripplingly depressed, you want the will to live and get out of bed in the morning, not to be a danger to yourself locked in a psych ward, but wouldn't it be strange to *never* feel mildly depressed again? Do you know who you are and how your emotions work without it?

So I don't aim for *symptom free* but for balance. Anxiety can have me rocking in the fetal position on the floor fixated on death, or it can motivate me to do only my best work. The obsession with structure and routine I get from autism can make me resistant to positive changes and a nightmare to improvise with, or a productive, efficient person who's hard to sidetrack for long. Maladaptive daydreaming can take over my life and have days pass where I externally mostly stare at the wall, or it can make me a creative, prolific writer.

Some symptoms I could maybe do without. I'm not really sure what sensory overload/processing issues get me if I could isolate it, but also you can't isolate it, and I'd keep the sensory *seeking,* I suppose.

I err my balancing act on the side of healthy, happy, and functional, as logic tells me to do, but sometimes I kind of miss the other side. I don't like to visit it for long, and the reality of it isn't just the romanticized tortured artist but a lot of actual grief, fear, guilt, exhaustion, and loneliness. You probably wouldn't want to *live* on a roller coaster, would you? Still, it gives that rush. It stocks the creative well.

So I'll take the Seroquel, but would I take the magic cure all pill? Not a chance.

PERSON FIRST LANGUAGE: BUT WHO AM I WITHOUT SCHIZOPHRENIA?

The thing with mental illness is that *it's all in your head* and *it's not who you are*. And, well, yes, it *is* all in your head, but your head is a pretty important place, and if we scientifically consider the brain the center of who you are, then isn't any long term major mental illness, you know, a part of who you are?

Person first language comes up a lot, the idea that you should say, as an example, *a person with schizophrenia,* not *a schizophrenic (person),* because they are first and foremost a person, not their disorder, disability, so on. I don't like person first language for myself, because I think it misses the point for me. I *am* a schizophrenic, just as much as I am a daughter, a wife, a writer, so on. You wouldn't use person first language to say I am *a person who writes* or *a person who is a writer,* would you? You'd just say *a writer.*

So then you have to ask the question: *when* do you use first person language, and what does it imply? Separation of the descriptor and identity? I am *a person who writes* because I pick up a pen now and then, but I am *a writer* because I identify as one, spend a significant amount of time on it, care about it that much. Okay, but I *identify* as a schizophrenic, too. It's a part of who I am just as much, if not more. So what does the assumption of using person first language for it *really* imply to me? That it's something I *shouldn't* identify with, that you *assume* I don't want to identify with it. It's just as much an assumption as saying *a schizophrenic,* and it tries to decide *for me* what my identity should be.

I don't speak for all schizophrenic people here, only for myself. I know some others *do* consider it solely a negative (and I still endorse seeking treatment to achieve your desired balance in any case), and it's had much more devastating effects on their lives than it's had on mine. Though, I will throw out there: so have a lot of identities. Should I stop saying I am *a daughter* because others might be the victims of child abuse?

So if I identify as *a schizophrenic,* there's the question of *if* there is a difference between my self and my schizophrenia. I don't think there's any more of a separation point there than between my self and my writing, and ultimately I believe that what deserves a place as part of one's true *identity* (rather than a list of traits or roles they've ever exhibited) is something that's up to the individual. There's the whole *keep your identity small* concept.

But let's examine it for a minute. Who am I, without schizophrenia?

My personality definitely would change based on a

lack of paranoia (being a paranoid schizophrenic). Even in periods between more complete delusion, there's… traits. Without assuming negative intentions from others, I'd probably be more open minded and perhaps make more friends, and make fewer snap judgments (though, largely, my snap judgments are pretty good, so I don't know if that part actually turns out any better for me). I'd probably then exhibit traits of the different pool of people I'd associate with over time, the whole *you are the average of the five people you spend the most time with* concept.

If I was less on edge, if I didn't have the constant *there's someone behind me* feeling and obsession with death, I'd presumably be more relaxed, but perhaps less productive. Quirks of mine around security might slip away, with or without consequence.

If I didn't have negative, insulting voices floating around my head now and then, I might develop higher self esteem and self sabotage less (though this isn't *too* much of an issue currently).

If psychosis didn't—shall we say *enhance*—my PTSD symptoms (flashbacks that are really hallucinations, hypervigilance *plus* paranoia) among others (the autism, the anxiety, and yes, those are part of my identity, too), those would probably drastically change, be less gripping.

Without negative symptoms (loss of interest in everyday activities, social withdrawal), I would probably be less hyperfocused on the things that never lose my obsessive interest (say, writing), and more interested in the little dopamine boosts of playing a game or watching a movie together, which I usually lightly resist or at least don't usually truly care for. This might be less productive, but a big mood changer, and, while I'm still an extrovert, it would have a huge impact on my ability to maintain acquaintances and turn them into friends, and engage in normal buffer activities, rather than my *"converse for twelve straight hours, maybe over food* or alternatively *parallel play/work* and almost nothing in between" approach.

Having a firmer relationship with reality would probably bring my daydreaming out of the maladaptive/dissociative category, as I believe those are highly connected for me, daydreams no longer taking over my reality and replacing it, just being something that still *feels* inside my head, or at least *picture in picture* style visualization. This would completely change my writing process as I know it, as it's been observed that most of it is my characters running wild in my daydreams—controlling me far more than I control them, both in demanding my attention, and in the way I absorb their traits—until something coherent and gripping happens to emerge (largely beyond my conscious control). Then, it's just a matter of getting paper and making some last minute adjustments. Removing schizophrenia also removes writing as I know it.

Gee… does that all sound like a major personality/identity change to you guys, too? Even more than removing, say, my identity as a writer?

So, yes, schizophrenia *is* also a part of my identity, I get to decide that, and I'll also talk about it as such.

BECOMING YOUR CHARACTERS, FOR BETTER OR WORSE: A SCHIZOPHRENIC AUTHOR AND THE REAL WORLD

I've encountered a lot of *firsts* while writing *the I'll Give You series*, as it's been my first fiction project of any length since I started working on the ever ongoing *Contrivance* in 2011. I've had a lot of fun getting to really know new characters for the first time in a long time, though I had kind of forgotten about their capacity to surprise me.

Over six months into writing the series, after having published the first book, one of the four main characters (and, mind you, there were only supposed to be *two* main characters at first, and this one wasn't one of them) informed me, in the way that fictional characters do for me—a mix of the typical creative type and the schizophrenic—that she'd had an eating disorder this entire time. Was formerly anorexic/occasionally still struggled, specifically.

I looked back over every instance in the series concerning this character and food. Yup. Body type: hmm. Looked at her risk factors: unprocessed trauma, a dancer in profession, a sometimes perfectionistic self destruction type... yeah, there it all was.

Interestingly, it was one of the branches of disorder I had the least experience with and least knowledge about. And I usually stuck closer to writing what I knew in that regard. Still, I started research, the clinical I was largely unfamiliar with, but also finding some personal accounts of others. I took a few online eating disorder assessments to get a feel for the key symptoms and treatment process, but of course I had amply healthy, normal scores, no indicators.

I wove it quietly into the background of the story. Even when mental health got explored as a main theme, it tended to stay in the background, not the main issue we were dealing with and mostly... ish... a piece from backstory.

Still, it informed a lot, lived in the background, and sometimes got brought up in companion pieces. Certainly it was in my head, even as research slowed.

Almost another year later, I was still writing, publishing book two and starting book three, but also fielding a few concerns building in my head, noting developing obsessions and tendencies over the last year, on and off phases becoming more *on* than *off*. I took the assessments I'd taken early on in research a second time. This time, my scores had almost skyrocketed, all *on the border* or *in the mild range* of disordered eating.

Specifically, I had key anorexia symptoms—religiously counting and often restricting calories, fasting entirely, constantly weighing myself, sometimes upping my daily exercise, even getting into a purging behavior or two— though my BMI still hovered in the low end of the healthy range. Picking up research again—more oriented towards virtual social spaces for those with eating disorders—I thought, *Me, too*, a lot, realizing I'd had a lot of the same disordered thoughts independently.

I couldn't feel too surprised. I'd seen this one coming, a little. (Note: I know such online assessments are not all strictly scientific. I'm just throwing it out there as anecdotal evidence.)

While stumbling through those assessment lists, I'd tried another one, this one for empathy. The score was out of a possible eighty, with scores below *thirty* indicating a lack of empathy common in people with autism. My wife did it, too, and scored a fifty-eight. I got *fourteen*.

While I'd foreseen picking up the symptoms of a character struggling with the remnants of a disorder I don't have, as a schizophrenic writer with a fine, fine line between *character* and *self*, often absorbing their traits, feelings, and symptoms, I remained a low empathy *person* in the real world, as noted on the paperwork when I was diagnosed with autism, and as shown by frustrated people in my life again and again.

I've talked to other neurodivergent creative types about their lines between *character* and *self* in depth for years. Even then, I experience it differently than almost anyone else I've met, aligning much more closely with people who experience psychosis, where the line is… blurrier. Thinner. Flexible.

I react more strongly to my characters' emotions: laughing, crying, tensing, smiling, heart racing in real time on their behalf, sometimes cathartically when I can't do it out of my *own* emotions. Yet I'm a poor mirror for other real people, slow to pick up on and respond to social cues, often read as a little flat and quiet, mostly by those who don't know me well.

I almost slowly *become* my characters, but fail to lean into the personalities of those around me as strongly. There's the adage that you're an average of the five people you're closest to. I think the people I spend time with can tell you a whole lot about me, but I honestly feel at any time more like an average of the five *characters* I've spent the most time writing recently, their personalities, interests, quirks, struggles, than the five people I've spent the most time with.

Now, this can be a two way street. Maybe as *I* shift in one direction or another, I relate more to one character or another, and spend more time writing them, though it often seems random. Maybe, a year ago, something in my brain was thinking a lot about neuroticism around weight loss, or food (some of which I've always had in sensory issues if nothing else) for *me*, and I projected it onto a character instead.

I might frequently project things onto characters before I realize, *Oh, that thought was for* me, absorbing the trait, emotion, interest, quirk, symptom, so on, myself, *later*, thinking that I first *got it* from that character I quickly assigned the initial thought to. All possible. Art imitates life; life imitates art. It is easier for me to reflect things already in my head in one way or another than reflect external, sentient people. Still, I really feel like the symptoms came later.

Regardless, I find it interesting. I'm mostly trying to consciously turn away from disordered eating/related behaviors, and not absorb that dangerous character element. I don't think I'm physically at much risk, but I've been really struggling with this mentally for quite a while now, and am trying to recognize that for me, it might just be an effect of psychosis, and treat it as such.

Still. Things to think about.

MY IMAGINARY DOG WANTS ME TO BE PSYCHOTIC: THE WAR BETWEEN CREATIVITY AND FUNCTIONALITY

I had a weird revelation the other day.

During one of my typical late night rambles—when I'm up that late—I was talking about the way I visualize and compartmentalize parts of my mind. The filing cabinets of thoughts and library of memories. "And, of course, there's Farrah's Void."

I have long wondered why Farrah, the puppy hallucination, appears to me again and again, the one question mark amongst other recurring hallucinations clearly based in trauma or the obvious.

Farrah often "appears" via somewhat mismatched

visual, auditory, and tactile hallucinations, and the sixth sense, for short spells of time. But there's one other mode of really feeling like I'm interacting with her: going to her Void.

It was more common when I first started hallucinating Farrah about a year and a half ago, around the one year anniversary of the event that gave me PTSD. I would dissociate, and rather than be in reality, or in one of my fictional worlds, or in a slightly alternate version of reality, I would "go to" Farrah's Void, an endless white abyss containing basically me, the dog, and occasionally an object I imagined. It looked and functioned a lot like Janet's Void from *The Good Place,* hence the nickname. It also got Farrah dubbed *my schizophrenia tamagotchi,* because it mimicked that pet-plus-blank-environment kind of game.

While I truly visit Farrah's Void less now—sure, I can picture Farrah or her Void any time I want, but that's not a true hallucination or dissociative experience—I *feel* like it's there, like the thought filing cabinets and the memory library. I explained it as, "I almost have *too* much object permanence." Dogs don't just appear and disappear, after all. Surely, Farrah (who's truly just a quirk of my brain chemicals) *goes* somewhere when she's not *with me,* here meaning, projected onto the real world.

Sometimes I *want* Farrah to come out and visit, so to speak, and I try to tempt her with normal imagining of her that doesn't stick like the hallucination, mental talk, *C'mere, puppy...,* and occasionally bribing her with a real piece of chicken or tennis ball, which I'm sure looks, y'know, totally sane to the outside observer.

But Farrah doesn't respond to these, obviously. She primarily appears when I am upset. At first I thought this was based on being a certain *level* of upset, and felt invalidated when she didn't appear at times/the right brain chemicals didn't happen. I wondered if she was a kind of psychotic, automatic self soothing mechanism, the free dopamine of a free puppy—and I still do think she nudges me towards a form of self soothing. Then I started tying her to more of a certain *kind* of upset. It had to run deep, be based in trauma, grief, existential loneliness, and already be a little dissociative or psychotic.

I humorously personified—puppy-ified?—her appearances to myself repeatedly, and in my ramble that night. Y'know, she has stuff to do in her Void, I guess. Balls to chase. Treats to eat. *Five more minutes, Mom.* She can't eat a *real* piece of chicken, anyway.

But trying to assign Farrah *motives*, the revelation hit me:

You're the part of my brain that wants to be psychotic and creative, and not sane/unimaginative.

Now, there is a whole spectrum in between those things, and I am often battling with where on it I should be. I believe that *psychosis* enhances my creativity; but I need *functionality* to deliver that creative energy in a consumable medium to the world.

Paranoia (as in, paranoid schizophrenia) keeps me on edge, reminds me that death comes for us all—not to mention the death trauma I hallucinate reliving over and over—and keeps me focused on the creative works that will outlive me… or hugging my knees and rocking in terror. Lack of connection to reality keeps me hyperfocused on both my fictional characters and on the *big* emotional rushes of publishing another book, and less interested in the minor rushes of board games and television shows and normal socialization, things I tend to write off as distractions… yet get you through the day and create friendships. My daydreams are dissociative, maladaptive, psychotic—my characters run free, in tighter and tighter spirals until something coherent and gripping happens to emerge without me, and then I rush for pen and paper… or remain trapped in a dissociative fugue on the floor.

There's a balance.

I tend to place medical professionals and the people who love me mostly on one side: functionality and happiness.

But that night, I realized who was on the other side: Farrah.

Previous mentions of Farrah on this blog are kind of damning. Hallucinating her herding me towards my notebook, or being upset when I decided to go back on antipsychotics—mostly as a mirror of my own emotions.

Yikes?

And yet I can't really blame that adorable little face (yes, she does make hallucinating tempting) for favoring psychosis, because there are days I favor it, too, days I romanticize the dysfunctional, the creative, the obsessive. But…

Okay, Farrah. I need my functionality; I need a touch of tortured artist syndrome. You don't win, but maybe I can meet you somewhere in the middle.

Wherever might be halfway between reality and your Void.

BEING A SCHIZOPHRENIC, CREATIVE TYPE DROPOUT

There's this memory that keeps coming to my mind recently.

I'm probably fifteen, and I'm sitting in my usual spot at the two lab tables pushed together, front and center, in my environmental science class, my program class/ major. We've just gotten our—I think—PSAT results, or some other big standardized test. There are so many of them. My friends chatter somewhat nervously about their already high scores around me.

I, sporting the ever present disheveled purple ponytail and bags under my eyes in the same color, the school fashion, am booting up my class notes on my school Google Drive account in one tab, and whatever writing project in the other. I usually work on both simultaneously, noting down the slide, then turning to my writing, evoking good natured teasing from our teacher as the others scramble to get the notes in. My overstuffed backpack beside me contains school supplies, several leisure books, a four hundred page binder printout of my latest NaNoWriMo novel, and Xanax. We're all on Xanax. The class bearded dragon settles into the hood on my jacket.

"Whatever, we all know Hannah did best," my friend E says, of the scores. She's the one not on Xanax; she's on Adderall, and I hear any extras are a hot commodity. She snatches the oversized envelope out of where it still rests in my hand. She swears loudly, then snaps her gum, earning a halfhearted:

"Hey," from our teacher.

Everyone peers at my results and makes similar remarks. J, not sharing her exact results, squirms; she doesn't test well. I squeeze her shoulder. I'm kind of in love with her anyway.

I hang out with the somewhat nerdy kids, in an extremely selective magnet school, and they are wowed. Their scores are *good.* They are *by the time you take your actual SATs, your scores might get you into the Ivy League* good. Even J will go to a very nice college. M, currently muttering, "Jesus Christ, *ninety-ninth* percentile?" is a talented swimmer, always arriving to class dripping wet after waking well before dawn. Their percentiles are in the upper eighties, low nineties.

But my scores are best, as E predicted. Because I'm Hannah, and I'm the smartest, and I'm ambitious, and I get all the plaudits, and I write books, and I'm *going places*, and I haven't really slept in years.

The funny thing about this memory is that I am, to my knowledge, the only one who doesn't technically graduate.

I effectively drop out just a few months later.

Here's another memory.

Ultimately, after exploring options, I had opted to write my own curriculum plan and "homeschool" myself for a year (read: run around the arts district with the local NaNoWriMo group), then get my high school equivalency a year early. I'd already worn out public school, private school, magnet school, and online school. I'd now attempted a few community college classes, mostly online, without much enthusiasm or success. Depending on how I tell this story, I either had a psychotic break and dropped out of high school, graduated a year early after opting to be an autodidact homeschooler for a year, or I left to pursue my greater passions/"creative differences".

Now, though, aged nineteen, I was sitting in the hallway near my Anthropology class on a dreary morning in Cambridge, MA. I'd somehow gotten into a lovely, small, private liberal arts college with a very nice scholarship. It was a great school in a lot of ways, and I was in love with the greater Boston area (and maybe yet another girl). But by October, I was in a seventy-two hour psych hold, and after almost going home to Vegas (recently rattled by the October 1 shooting), I had opted to stay. Adjust my course load, work with the counseling center and disability office, change my meds, get myself together, and try again.

As I sat in the hall, staring at my notebook, too drained to write, early to class simply because I had nowhere better to be, I dreaded going into the classroom. I dreaded sitting through the lesson. I dreaded sprinting to Arts and Social Justice on a different campus immediately after, and sitting through that. I dreaded the idea of going back to my tiny, sixth floor walkup dorm, and doing homework with my roommate.

I could not *comprehend* how badly I did not want to go to that class.

And as I sat there, it dawned on me that I had never really wanted to go to that class, or to Arts and Social Justice, or to any other class. There were ones I liked better and worse, had more or less passion for the subject, and got on with the professor better or worse. But while I loved learning, the subjects in theory, I had never really wanted to go, never really wanted to do the homework.

Why was I going to college?

I just wanted to write, mostly. *And what do you do with a degree in creative writing?* Most of the courses I'd ever taken seemed to just be beating my will and creativity out of me. I had just dropped my planned second major, a self designed program in conlanging expressive arts therapy, realizing, after my psych ward stay—where I'd done the most productive writing since I'd arrived in Cambridge— that I could never work in mental health. I was thinking about doing the dual degree program, getting a Master's because it sounded good, but why? I didn't need a degree to write a book. I'd written several. This wasn't actually any better than my community college classes online, and it cost a lot more: money, time, creative energy, sanity, being away from home. I hadn't even wanted to finish high school.

I... don't want to be here.

I had never really *wanted* to go to college, in reality. It just seemed like a thing to do. I wanted the *experience*. I liked sitting around with my favorite professors over lunch, discussing this book and that. I liked forming a schedule around interesting sounding subjects. I liked creating pretty study guides, and even studying them, not to test, but to learn. I liked the culture of study groups, of library and museum trips. I liked learning, I liked reading, I liked writing. But I had almost never… liked *school.*

I didn't walk into my Anthropology class.

I stood, turned around, walked out of the building, and was at the airport less than eight hours later.

After that, I started one more part time community college semester online just to appease those who asked, "But what are you doing with your life?" It got dropped when I became too ill with what turned out to be mold poisoning, and I didn't look back. After sorting out the mold, getting a relevant surgery, so on, well, that was when Dad died. And suddenly I was making money, a landlord, and the fact that I spent all day writing and being a housewife (finally fell in love with the right girl who wanted what I did) suddenly seemed valid.

So I felt like I could focus on that: being a housewife with my own projects. I published several books, and translated my nonfiction into becoming an alternative sexuality educator. I started taking a self paced online butler school course I was actually passionate about, couldn't imagine dropping not matter how challenging it got. I talked about books with friends and did challenges together and journaled and volunteered at the library and learned and read and wrote.

And, no real regrets. School wasn't for me. It's for some people. But not for me. I found enough happiness and health and success and knowledge elsewhere.

I think a lot of people think of me as the academic, educated sort, using obscure vocabulary words and always having my face in a book or journal, teaching and learning. But really, I'm a high school dropout who hasn't loved school since the fifth grade.

And I'm more than okay with that.

THE LIMITATIONS OF TRANSLATING DAYDREAMS TO OTHER MEDIUMS

The other night at dinner, my wife and I were talking about doomsday prepping, and I joked that, if caught unprepared and possibly alone, my end of the world plan would be to go befriend the nearest preppers, go full Scheherazade, and become the group storyteller. They can't just steal my supplies, they can't really have me teach them my One Useful Skill and then kill me; I can't be replaced by technology. I need to be alive and coherent, and the apocalypse is actually rather boring. And I have an endless well of material. Gonna go have a minor psychotic break. Be right back with new plotlines.

Really, I think that is my grand backup plan in a lot of ways. No matter what happens in the real world, I have that endless well in my head to retreat to. I spent a decent amount of the height of quarantine staring into space while off in those worlds (and then books got published about them—after I went back on meds). Nothing can destroy that. Too much Seroquel can definitely diminish

the extent to which it can replace reality,
turn *dissociative* and *maladaptive* into *creative* and *publish able*, but a decent portion *is* just the writer in me, not psychosis.

And let's be real, where am I getting all this Seroquel after doomsday?

A few days later, I was scrolling the app store. I'm a digital minimalist (and a minimalist, period), but I was pondering what to use the iPad I perpetually struggle to use or get rid of for, and I got it set up again. Then, I ended up browsing the app store after downloading my small handful of go tos, seeing what was new for iPads. I was reminded of Minecraft (which I played briefly in 2016 or so) and The Sims 4 (I was big into The Sims 2 and 3 as a kid; I downloaded The Sims 4 on sale several months back, but other than playing around with making a few characters and checking out changes, didn't do much and uninstalled it before it became a distraction). I'm trying to remain a minimalist but be a little less neurotic, and considered giving one game or the other or both another go in my downtime.

And I might. But at that moment, I remembered the limitations of the games I'd been not so much frustrated by, but bored with. By nature of being an app, there are limitations. It is an incredible amount of work if not impossible to recreate the detail of settings or characters in my head pixel by pixel, not to mention limited choices of actions, little real dialogue, and how many things are narration or feelings or inner monologue. It also lacks the touch, taste, smell, other sensory elements that I experience off in my head. Sometimes the limitations are a good creative challenge, a way to have to mix things up a little, get out of exactly the script I'm thinking of to see what might happen if something I'd taken for granted *had* to be tweaked. At other times, all I can think is: why would I use an app for something I can do better with my eyes closed?

As a kid, I liked The Sims, as mentioned. I usually filled in the rest of the details in my head, though, going for simple in the game. I also didn't recreate my writing as much as you'd expect, choosing new characters, settings, and plotlines to play out that were better suited to the game's strengths and weaknesses.

I looked back at my notebook. I thought of drawing, or writing. I can't really draw much—I've spent time each day this year trying to learn, but it's slow learning, and slow to create, for me. I do believe that anyone can learn to draw if they really set their mind to it, but I just don't have the passion for it to do so, and I do have some serious spatial reasoning issues. And I still ultimately get stills that are limited by the tools I'm using.

Writing, of course, my true creative love, is my medium of choice. But I thought more, and, really, that has its limits, too. It's just the set of limits I'm most okay with. That I must use words to describe everything— I don't have visuals or audio, powers of scent or taste or touch. That I only speak English fluently, that there isn't a word for every incredibly specific thing, no matter what those fascinating words lists might have you think. I push at the limits of punctuation and grammar and word usage. There's the fact that, in my head, my characters have specific voices, and I'm not going to redescribe—or manage to describe—*exactly* what they sound like every time they speak, nor *exactly* what they look like or are wearing, or that their skin is exactly this level of dry, or that they use exactly this imagined fruity scent of bath products, or that their favorite shirt has that soft texture of having gone through the wash a thousand times.

There are also a lot of things that happen in my head that I can't describe because it doesn't actually *work* that way—my daydreams work more like dreams at times, not to mention being slightly beyond my control, and might not make sense according to laws of physics or reason. What shirt they're wearing might flip flop in my mental vision based on the tone of the scene, but it's unrealistic that they're running in and out of the room to change their shirt based on the tone of conversation. A sequence might be perfect in my head, but when I try to write it out, I realize it might require someone to have their hands in three places at once, whether it's combat or erotica.

And I can't capture *everything* perfectly every time, so I need to figure out what is important, what is good enough, this time. A literal bomb could be going off in the story, but the *important* detail might be that a character's eyes flicked to the site of the explosion right before it happened, an implication that they knew it was coming. I need to pick that out from the mental vision, not a description of the explosion. It might be worthwhile to give an idea of a character's general fashion sense or even what they're wearing in a particular scene, but not to mention every time they change their socks, unless that's something that really says something about them, because they're always changing their socks, or they never change their socks, or they have a very distinct taste in socks. Even writing a novel still feels like creating an outline, in a way.

But, I find it a worthy challenge.

VACATION MEMORIES, OR NOT: EARLY SIGNS OF PSYCHOSIS

When I was fourteen, my mom and I took a trip to New Jersey. We visited family and friends, saw some sights, all that good stuff. It was a great trip in a lot of ways and I have fond memories of it. I reminisced about it to my wife recently, and I recalled two things I frequently think of from that trip that go beyond vacation memories and into Things To Ponder territory.

One:

It was a several hour long flight to get there, and to be honest, I don't remember much of it, but it meant a lot of transportation downtime, which means I was probably doing a lot of daydreaming. Many of my best plotlines and revelations were born of this kind of time. The earliest born recognizable plotline from the final version of *Contrivance* (which I published recently) was born on a roadtrip to California for my wife's job. Another important revelation, same project, on a roadtrip back from a Lake Tahoe vacation with family and friends. I reframed "What Happened Last Storm" on the way to San Francisco (which was reposted recently).

Anyway, after the flight, I believe we went straight to visit my grandparents, the primary reason for the trip. And after that is the part that I remember clearly. Let me tell you this: there is not a single left turn in the state of New Jersey. I am sure of it. I am pretty sure we had to go to New York to turn around after missing the (okay, one) left turn to get to our hotel. So it was a long drive.

Apparently fresh out of the usual daydreaming material, my mind began to wander further. Daydreams started to wander a little too far ahead of my conscious thought train, and I abruptly slammed on the mental brakes.

Where did that *come from?*

The daydream train had deviated from what would ever truly be canon for the nascent project. Into vaguely uncomfortable territory I couldn't really identify at the time. It was far from a sexual fantasy or anything, but something about it had the flashing warning light of *don't think that.* I'd now file it somewhere in the alternative lifestyle category. But I'd barely even heard those words at the time. And, interestingly, a lot of my daydreams already went into what I would now call that category, going as far back as I can remember, to my earliest memories. So why was I suddenly worried at that moment? Doing the same plotline with new characters? Fledgling awareness of the taboo? Or increased paranoia?

I believe the important thing isn't the content of the daydream—honestly, I don't remember the details—but the slamming on the mental breaks, the *don't think that.* Thought policing myself. I stopped daydreaming and sat there in the car and pondered that. Why *was* I policing my own thoughts? Did I believe others around me could hear them? That some form of God could hear them? That bad thoughts inevitably led to bad actions? (There's also probably a whole post's worth on *why did I instinctively feel that content was taboo while barely understanding it?*, but that may be better suited to a different blog.)

I decided, sitting there and reasoning with myself, that I supposed there *wasn't* a reason I should police my thoughts. And I indulged the daydream and mentally crept forward. Still, I found myself slamming the brakes on daydreams like that under various circumstances. If I was alone and someone entered the space, I slammed on the brakes, like abruptly closing embarrassing computer tabs when you realize someone's standing behind you. So on. Now, I wasn't very good at the brake slamming—that's kind of the maladaptive part—but, I tried.

This whole thing resonates a lot with—well, a) maladaptive and dissociative daydreaming perhaps over the edge of psychosis in itself, but I talk about that going back to my earliest memories a lot here, but also b) paranoia—as in, paranoid schizophrenia, one of my eventual diagnoses. That paranoia—the thought policing —creeps in to this day, though I have so few secrets these days, even if I believe someone can hear my thoughts, I don't actually worry about much.

Here's the interesting thing: I had only in the past six months or so, at the time of the trip, been diagnosed with so much as anxiety. I had no known psychotic symptoms at the time. When I started on medication for the anxiety, my dad even reacted badly to the first prescription recommended, because it was technically an antipsychotic. He thought this whole thing was already getting out of hand. I'd gone from "a little too stressed out" to "psychotic" in no time at all in this psychiatrist's eyes (even though it'd been explained that the psychiatrist understood I had only anxiety and was giving me this drug to treat me for anxiety and sleep, no matter the primary use of it). Point being, I was not psychotic at the time. Or, so we believed? And I was early onset as it was—definitive psychotic symptoms around the time I turned fifteen, diagnosed at seventeen. The average onset for schizophrenia in women is the late twenties to early thirties.

But some of my symptoms do go further back than even my anxiety diagnosis (which, to be fair, may have been long overdue).

Exhibit two from that trip:

My mom and I went to the Museum of Natural History. I hear it's a really cool museum. Here's the problem: I have no memory of it.

I remember going into NYC from New Jersey. It was my first time on a subway, all that fun stuff. I even remember arriving at the museum and I believe having food in the cafeteria. Then my memory cuts out. Then, we're standing on the front steps of the museum on the way to meet a friend of Mom's for food. I am having a panic attack because something went wrong on the camera and it deleted all of our many photos of the experience.

Now, that sucks for both of us and all—but I'm long over that part—I was just prone to such panic attacks at the time. (Sorry, Mom, for all of it.) But the interesting thing is I remember insisting that because there were no photos, it was like we hadn't been there at all. I was already struggling to recollect details that had seemed very clear a moment ago. My brain insisted that no evidence meant that it hadn't happened. The museum wasn't quite real. I don't think I expressed this very well, though. I didn't even understand that anxious thought process at the time. I don't remember what my memory of the museum was like closer to the event—I remember losing details as we walked away from it—but today at least, I've got nothing. I'm okay with that. A lot of memories fade, anyway. One day, I'll go back.

Now, today, if after very obviously living an experience for several hours, I lost the external evidence of it and spiraled into panic, thinking that the whole thing had never truly happened, I would probably think I was having an acute psychotic episode, and might even be able to articulate that. It would indicate an obvious loss of a sense of reality, unable to grasp the realness of something I had just experienced. A loss of permanence. Today, I frequently use photos to keep reality real, so to speak. They ground me and provide facts.

When I'm so consumed by the image of my father dead that I can no longer picture him alive, photos ground me. Photos say, *This is what he looked like.* I may or may not be in a mental state where my perception of the photos (selfies, candids, quick pictures, not things subjected to editing) is that they are undeniably fact, but something in the back of my mind always whispers, *They're right.*

My phone's photo feed provides me timelines, little moments that keep large stretches of time real. Throughout the early height of the pandemic, there are pictures of interesting animals I saw at the empty park, our cats, food I made, candids of our little family in the pool, empty shelves at stores, signs announcing closings, masks left in the street, craft projects, our plants—tiny reminders tied to a specific moment in time that mean *this whole year really happened.* Not a weird montage from a movie. We all probably feel that way about 2020 sometimes. I just feel like that a lot.

At the time of that trip, though, I didn't believe I was psychotic—although I knew very little about what psychosis truly was like. I certainly didn't know how to articulate any of that. But could it have been a subtle prodome symptom, an early warning sign? Maybe. My first definitive symptoms of psychosis came just six months later.

I suppose it's not that important now, but it's interesting to ponder looking back.

HOW TO BE AN ALLY TO PEOPLE WITH PSYCHOSIS

(This is heavily based off my class "Schizophrenia in the Scene", on how to be an ally to alternative sexuality practitioners with psychosis. I've adapted it in written form for a more general audience.)

So: how to be an ally to people with psychosis, in several contexts, by a schizophrenic.

Psychosis 101

It can be hard to be an ally if you don't know the basics. So let's go over a few things.

Psychotic Disorders

First, let's look at some of the most common types of psychotic disorders. We'll go over some more specifics in a bit.

• Schizophrenia. Schizophrenia is probably what you think of when you think of psychosis. It's the disorder I have. Symptoms include hallucinations, delusions, and negative symptoms. While the average onset is the late teens to early twenties for men and late twenties to early thirties for women, my symptoms officially appeared around the time I turned fifteen, and I was officially diagnosed at seventeen: early onset is possible, but it's extremely uncommon to be diagnosed under age twelve or over age forty.

• Schizoaffective disorder. Schizoaffective disorder is a disorder with chronic symptoms of both schizophrenia and a mood disorder (either bipolar—with manic and depressive episodes—or depression).

• Delusional disorder. Delusional disorder (formerly known as paranoid disorder) is defined by the presence of delusion, though they don't usually have as many behavioral symptoms. While hallucinations may be present, they are always related to the delusions.

There are other types of psychotic disorders, and other disorders that can have features of psychosis. For example, schizophreniform disorder has all of the symptoms of schizophrenia, but only lasts one to six months.

Types of Schizophrenia

Within that first diagnosis—schizophrenia—there are several subtypes. Here are some of the most common.

• Paranoid. This is one you've probably heard of, and it's the kind I have. It's defined by unreasonable suspicion and paranoid delusions.

• Disorganized. Disorganized thoughts, speech, and behaviors. These symptoms tend to appear in all kinds of schizophrenia, but especially here. Thinking may feel complicated, and speech may come out as *word salad*, or gibberish. People with disorganized schizophrenia may have strange physical quirks or a lack of certain mannerisms at all, or mirror the person they're with. Hallucinations and delusions tend to be less pronounced.

• Catatonic. This type is defined by catatonia— appearing to be in a frozen, statue like state (silent, still, staring, etc.) I've also experienced this episodically— primarily early on. Or, you may experience random hyperactivity (fidgeting, mirroring the person you're with).

(Note: I've seen that the correct phrasing has technically changed from, say, *paranoid schizophrenia* to *schizophrenia with paranoid features*. So bear that in mind, but I'll say I'm not super fond of that phrasing. As someone with a lot of catatonic symptoms at times, I used to say things like *paranoid schizophrenia with catatonic features*. So what now?)

Symptoms

I've mentioned many symptoms above, but let's dive into what they really mean.

• Hallucinations. Hallucinations involve seeing, hearing, tasting, feeling, smelling, generally sensing something that isn't there. While hearing voices is commonly referenced, hallucinations can involve all senses and also include object *distortions* (think Alice in Wonderland), and be more or less vivid. You may or may not know you're hallucinating. I experience all of this, and also have specific recurring hallucinations.

• Delusions. A delusion is something you believe that isn't true. You may believe that someone is out to get you (paranoid) or that you're actually someone famous (grandiose). You may not believe it in full—just have it as an intrusive thought you can't get rid of—or you may believe it entirely. I tend to have these episodically—usually triggered by a change I'm not expecting, like an object not being where I expect it to be, or vice versa—and generally be paranoid. Some delusions or categories have their own names, like grandiose or paranoid delusions, or Cotard's delusion.

  • Disorganized speech and behaviors. As mentioned, disorganized speech—*word salad*/gibberish that may sound coherent to the speaker, but not the listener (sometimes coming from disorganized *thoughts*) or going nonverbal—and disorganized behaviors (freezing, fidgeting, staring, flat affect/monotone, mirroring/parroting) can occur as part of psychosis. I experience these at times, especially when I get too tired. A lot of these also cross over with autism for me.

  • Negative symptoms. Negative symptoms are a lack of usual functions. This can mean executive dysfunction —struggling with normal self care, jobs, study, and activities. This can also mean flat affect and social withdrawal. This can also mean a lack of the ability to feel joy or feel interested in something. I also experience these, up and down.

Treatment

So, if someone is experiencing psychosis—what now?
  • Medication/antipsychotics. The front line treatment for psychosis is medication. You cannot truly treat psychosis with counseling or therapy alone. Medications designed to treat psychosis are called *antipsychotics* and come in many forms. With a psychiatrist's supervision,

you might try several before you find the med(s) and
dosage(s) that work best for you, keeping an eye out for
side effects. I take my antipsychotic med as a pill at night
(it also helps with sleep). Other meds might be useful,
and antipsychotics can also treat nonpsychotic disorders.
I was on some antipsychotics before I experienced
psychosis, for anxiety and sleep.

• Therapy. Therapy can still be useful to help *cope* with
psychotic symptoms and any other issues or disorders.
For meds and especially for therapy, the key is to get
the right one. Get the right medication (or combo),
and the right therapist. Not every therapist is someone
qualified to treat schizophrenia, someone you'll get along
with, or even very good at all—some can actively make
things *worse*. I've seen many. Make sure you find someone
qualified, who you like and you think really helps you.
It's not necessary, but it can be very valuable. I was in and
out of therapy from 2012 to 2020. I've been out since, but
have considered going back if I could, well, find the right
therapist.

• Psychosocial approach. This is a therapy like
approach that focuses on functioning in the world with
psychosis, including family education and counseling,
social skills training, occupational therapy, help with
accommodations at school or work, and being as
independent as possible (transportation, housing, etc.)

Interactions

Now that we've covered some basics, let's talk about how
to interact with someone who experiences psychosis,
whether they're talking about the experience or
struggling right now.

• First thing's first: don't assume you'd know if that person experiences psychosis. Don't invalidate them by saying things like *well, it's clearly not that bad* or *no, you don't.* They would know better than you do. Also, stay away from lines like *oh, I wouldn't have guessed* —it's not necessarily your business, and that may or may not actually be a compliment; it can sometimes feel invalidating that it's not apparent. Framing it as a *compliment* that it's not apparent can also be a form of shaming the invisible symptoms. Also, don't assume that the person is high functioning, not struggling, or even having a good day just because they're having a nice interaction with you. You don't know what they're going through. I get this a lot as someone who passes as "high functioning" most of the time.

• Don't treat it as extreme. Psychosis is often seen as *the deep end* of mental illness. While there are some valid reasons for it, don't use this as an excuse to be *othering*. It doesn't always feel great when someone says "you can *even* live a normal life with psychosis" or makes a comment to someone else like "at least you're not psychotic".

• Don't stereotype. Not all people who experience psychosis experience it the same way, to the same extent, or are the same person, or feel the same way about it. Don't lump everyone in together, and don't throw things under the psychosis label that have nothing to do with psychosis, like certain political beliefs.

• It's not a magic power. Please, do *not* tell people who experience psychosis that it's a magic power, a religious calling, a spiritual experience, that they're psychic, that they can see the future, the past, things you can't, another lifetime, just—any of it. If it belongs in a house of worship or a science fiction/fantasy novel, just don't say it. It can lead to an acute psychotic episode and fuel delusions and hallucinations. Whatever you believe, please keep it to yourself in this case.

• However, keep in mind that not everyone thinks their psychosis is all bad. I've written before on why I wouldn't cure my own schizophrenia if I could, and view it as a crucial part of my creative work. Don't force this as toxic positivity onto someone, but don't necessarily go, "Oh, that must be so horrible, I'm so sorry," either.

• Be aware of common psychosis triggers. As mentioned above, religion/spirituality/science fiction/fantasy kind of elements can be a big one. They also might be a special interest of that person's—I love talking about those things at times—but tread carefully, ask first, and if they're not up to it that day, they're not up to it that day, even if it's their favorite thing at other times. Other things: conspiracy theories, anything reminiscent of *The Matrix* or *Inception*, any "it was all a dream/simulation" etc., absurdist humor ("Cat? I don't see a cat," when there's a cat right in front of you.) And if they ask you to stop, *do it right away*. Don't continue on with the subject. Don't try to explain it. Don't apologize over and over; it puts the burden on them to keep interacting about this subject. *Move on*. It's probably already a little late.

• Stay neutral on delusions. Don't confirm them— they're not true, and this makes them harder to shake. It also makes *you* a known bad source of information if that person comes out of the delusion later. Don't deny them while the person is in them—this will just lead to frustration and confusion. Stay neutral. *"I understand you think that."* I've had delusions that the person I was talking to didn't exist/was a hallucination. I know it can be hard to stay neutral, but it's always better to nod and smile and stall a little if need be than to take a side.

• Reality checks (and why they probably don't work). Look, trying to reality check a hallucination is much more complex than you think it is. First, you'd have to check *all* five/more of your senses. Check every single thing affecting those senses in the environment, every object. Check if all of those things are oriented properly, the correct size, color, texture, distance—you get the idea. "You see the cup, too?" "Yes." But it's a completely different size to them. Flash of light? Well, maybe you just missed it—or maybe they're hallucinating. "Can you touch it?" Well, yes, sometimes visual and tactile hallucinations do line up. Hallucinations can also distort things like reflections and pictures; these may or may not function as reality checks. This tends to be a powerful instinct for people—reality checking—but proceed with caution. One yes to, "You see X, too?" doesn't mean the person is necessarily psychosis free. (Life hack: good noise cancelling headphones = auditory hallucination check.)

• Say what you mean. On both sides. Remember that words mean different things to different people. For example, my wife and I discovered that when she said, "I'm tired," she meant she had the vague urge to go lie down and rest. When I said, "I'm tired," I meant that I was a few minutes at most from blacking out/was a fall risk/"Catch me." That can be a pretty important distinction for a word people use all the time.

• Person-first language. Person first language (ex: *a person with schizophrenia* rather than *a schizophrenic person* or *a schizophrenic*) is commonly praised as a good default. And it is. But if it's not that person's preference, it's not that person's preference, and you should respect that, just as they/them are good default pronouns, but once someone tells you their preferred pronouns, you should use their preferred pronouns. And beware of clearly awkwardly rearranging a sentence around first person language, making it a bigger deal than it is. Think of this: if you wanted to say I was a writer, you'd probably just say, "Hannah's a writer," right? You wouldn't clumsily tiptoe around *Hannah is a person who writes*, because it's no big deal that being a writer is part of my identity. But psychosis probably trips your "I should use person-first language for this" button if you have one of those. But why? Are you deciding *for* me that it's not part of my identity, or that it *shouldn't* be something I identify with? Tread carefully here, and use the preference of the person in question.

Events/Groups

Considerations for event planning and social groups.

• Be honest (about your scope). If you're running anything that calls itself a support group, a safe space, a mental health/illness space, therapeutic, things like that: be very honest about what you can actually support. If you say you welcome all neurodivergent people, remember that it covers *anyone* who's not neurotypical, not "anxiety, depression, autism, ADHD, trauma". If you're not actually equipped to handle someone with psychosis—just be honest. It's much better for me to read in advance that an event or group is not meant for me (in a non judgmental way) than to show up and get all of the mistakes from the section above, which are very common in groups that are just not prepared.

- Sensory overload. For people with psychosis and many other mental illnesses, sensory overload is a real thing at events. Consider adequate, non flashing, neutral lighting, a quiet space with limited background noise, a lack of strong scents, etc.—or at least a space at your event where someone overwhelmed by those things can catch a break or socialize more easily. In the case of psychosis, sensory overload can also start with sensory experiences that only that person is experiencing—what might not seem like a lot to you, could be the straw that broke the camel's back.

- Physical safety. If there are steps, loose cords, things like that, in your event space, where your usual recommendation is *watch your step*, or things that require being very cognizant of your surroundings—see if there's a way you can make that safer for those who might not be so easily in touch with reality. If I'm dissociating, I'm not watching my step. Or, objects may be distorted or hidden by hallucinations. Maybe a spare shelf can double as a ramp on a step or two down into a living room pit, or you can tape those wires down securely.

- Privacy. If someone reaches out to you about being a group member with psychosis, keep it confidential unless they explicitly tell you otherwise. Just because they're telling you doesn't mean they're "out". Be willing to talk about related concerns privately. At an event, places where guests could get a moment alone or with a trusted loved one are very welcome if someone needs a minute to calm down.

- Reach out. Ask what you can do to make your event more accessible—with the opportunity for private, anonymous answers. Without being pushy, reach out to group members who have been quiet lately; maybe they just need a nudge or a reminder that they're welcome.

Relationships

Considerations for family, partners, close friends, etc.
  • Advanced (mental) health directives/power of attorney. These are documents that (at least where I am; there may be different versions available where you live) outline the healthcare you would like to receive (or not) in advance, and who can make decisions for you if you cannot make them for yourself. Consider adding people you trust here.
  • Emergency contact. Adding trusted loved ones as your emergency contact(s) at work/school/etc., and vice versa. Also, keeping a card in your wallet of your important medical information (medications, conditions, allergies, etc.) and emergency contacts (name, relation, phone number) can be a life saver. It has gotten me out of a bad situation where I was nonverbal or catatonic more than once.
  • Subtle "help" cues. It might help to establish a way to cue your loved one in to the fact that you're having a problem, if they can't generally tell/you can't always communicate that with normal signs. It could be a subtle way to signal for help in public (or a visual in a loud room), a hand signal for if you're nonverbal, so on—or different ones with different meanings.
  I hope this information helps out a little.

WANT TO KNOW ABOUT SCHIZOPHRENIA? ASK A SCHIZOPHRENIC

Recently, I taught for my first conference. In advance of the event, an organizer posted class highlights—the details of a particular class offered at the conference—regularly on social media. The comments section was usually quiet, maybe positive.

As it happened, one day I stumbled across a class highlight where the comments section wasn't going so well. It took me a second to realize that the class highlighted was mine.

My qualification was questioned, despite being in the post. It was a class on being an ally to alternative sexuality practitioners with schizophrenia. My qualification was being an alternative sexuality practitioner with schizophrenia.

The organizers had stated in many places that the conference presenters were mostly not mental health professionals. Most of us taught from our own experience. More was explained in the comments section. I didn't know the commenter, so it wasn't personal.

So why was I the only one who had this issue?

Probably: I was teaching the only class at the conference about psychosis.

The commenter cited that one could do a lot of harm, responding to psychosis without knowing what one was doing. And that's very true—that's a main reason I teach that class. But that was true of almost any subject at the conference. What I saw implicitly referenced was the *seriousness* of psychosis, or rather, the stigma. Even within a class list for a conference on mental health and alternative sexuality.

The stigma particular to psychosis is real.

But, okay, let's go with it for a second.

Does having schizophrenia make me qualified to write and teach about it (at this level)?

Yes. I think so.

Why?

Because, while it's subjective, I can tell you what schizophrenia feels like from inside it. Because all medical literature and research on schizophrenia relies on people like me being studied. Because even the average mental health professional can't give you first hand information on it.

Now, any diagnosis alone does not give me clear communication skills, or knowledge of the hard science, or so on. It just gives me experience to speak from—an experience that science studies and documents en masse, trying to figure out why, trying to figure out how to treat it, along with the physical tests and so on. I get other skills and knowledge from practice—teaching on many other subjects—and lots of research.

But I *am* qualified to talk about the first hand experience. Psychosis is in large part about your relationship with reality. Therefore, *my* perception of reality—versus *others'* perception of reality—at any given time, is half the picture.

You might see someone standing in the middle of the street, yelling and beating themselves with a lint roller until they bruise, or someone curled up motionless on the floor, staring at nothing, or someone calling an invisible dog and holding nothing like it's a leash, or someone vibrating in terror while fixated on an empty space in a bed, but I'm living something else.

I'm feeling the world crash down around me, I'm off in another world with my characters, I'm trying to get the whining dog to cooperate for once, I can see (and smell) the corpse in the bed. And that's a lot of context, and only I can fill that half in for sure.

Any mental illness, really, is, by nature, hard to get the full picture of from an external perspective alone.

And many schizophrenics struggle to share their perspective—it comes with the territory. On my bad days, I can't share mine. On other days, thankfully, I can.

But ultimately, if you want to know what schizophrenia is really like?

I'd ask a schizophrenic.

SUNDOWNING, AND DAYDREAMS VS. HALLUCINATIONS

Recently, I read *The Productivity Project* by Chris Bailey. It's a great book, and it emphasizes managing your time, attention, and energy. One of my key takeaways was to stop fighting my natural sleep patterns, to shift my schedule, and go to bed and wake up a little later, like my body wanted.

However, this meant sacrificing the hour of writing I had scheduled early in the morning, before brunch with my wife. This didn't feel like a huge loss, though. I frequently didn't get much done in that hour, when my body wanted to be asleep. I had to fight for every word, and it wasn't actually when most of my writing happened.

So, I looked to reschedule my official writing time according to the book's principles, figuring out when my energy naturally peaked. Except I realized that I didn't want to write at that time. I wanted to write when I had *less* energy, when the daydreams that fuel

my fiction are sleepier, more like full dreams. I wanted
to write at night, perhaps right *before* the daily dose of
my antipsychotic, when its concentration in my body
would theoretically be lowest. But not in the morning,
too tired to get words down at all—which also sometimes
happened at night—when my daydreams were too hazy,
not vividly dreamlike.

I ended up not structuring my writing time via
strict daily timeblocking at all, for now preferring the
flexibility of a monthly goal, the ability to separate
sleepy, creative, psychotic daydreaming/brainstorming
with pen loosely in hand and the part where I actually get
coherent paragraph after paragraph down on paper. But
it was an interesting observation.

I more recently started reading another
book: *Hallucinations* by Oliver Sacks. From that, I learned
about sundowning—a behavioral phenomenon that
occurs in people with Alzheimer's and other conditions.
It involves symptoms of confusion and distress that
start around sunset and continue through the night. It
can also cause hallucinations and occur in people with
psychosis.

I found that interesting, as someone who had recently
expressed a preference for at least brainstorming at night
—*because* my semipsychotic daydreams ranged closer
to full psychosis at that time. Even more so than in the
morning, when my daydreams didn't seem to have the
same grip despite my initial theory of low energy being
the important part. I also pondered the stereotype that
writers are night owls.

Additionally, I've long struggled with determining
what my daydreams *are.* Just a bit of creative type
syndrome? Maladaptive daydreaming? Part of my actual

psychosis? I've had a lot of creative type friends, though, and my daydreams don't work like theirs do, much more all consuming. They fit well into the maladaptive daydreaming category, but I still feel like they go a step further; I don't only struggle to control compulsively slipping into daydreams, but the *contents* of them also slip out of my grasp. Thus I have always defined them as semipsychotic, though they also don't fit the way I describe my more typical hallucinations.

But in reading *Hallucinations,* I stumbled across something else: the difference in eye movements between seeing, normal and maladaptive daydreams, hallucinations, and dreams. While your eyes tend to scan real areas and track real motion, most people's eyes go still—glaze over, zone out, if you will—when they are visualizing or daydreaming, unless maybe it's something very dynamic, or if it's scanning a visualization of certain kinds of information. In maladaptive daydreaming, this is also common, though some people sometimes truly act out the daydream, usually reserved for private situations. The eyes move—while eyelids are closed—when dreaming, during the REM (rapid eye movement) stage of sleep (current research suggests this is part of processing new/changing imagery, not scanning visuals in dreams).

When hallucinating, the eyes often move as if seeing something real. This has been studied a lot in terms of Charles Bonnet syndrome (visual hallucinations connected to loss of vision), as it has interesting implications about the difference—or lack thereof—in seeing versus *perceiving*.

So I tried a few informal experiments. I asked around, watching as others visualized/daydreamed, and asking what they saw when I did, and a few times, I sat in my office, left a recording Zoom meeting with just me in it open on my laptop in front of me, and sank into my daydreams, then watched the recordings and what my eyes did.

While I had no dramatic behaviors to note—I didn't fully act out the dream, and didn't do anything consciously—my eyes, always open, definitely moved. Remembering what I'd been daydreaming about, I noted that they sometimes tracked motion within the daydream, from roughly the perspective of the point of view character (all in third person, but kind of flipping back and forth at times the way the camera does in a movie)—following a character scrambling away in a chase. Or, my eyes acted out the way the observed character's eyes darted back and forth looking for a direction to run. Different bits.

But this helped confirm for me that my daydreams might go a bit *beyond*, and I was clearly able to observe that they did so more at night, in a way that made sense as a form of sundowning (among other evening symptoms—a heavier leaning towards more typical hallucinations, mood symptoms, dissociation, PTSD flashbacks, hypervigilance, the negative symptoms of schizophrenia, catatonia).

It can be very beneficial, validating, to find the word for something, a more objective way to look at it, to find out that other people do it, too, even for phenomena I had already casually observed.

So, I was glad to come across these things.

JULY 6TH

Today marks the three year anniversary of discovering
my father's death, and it's the little things, really.

I try to fall asleep the night before the anniversary. My
wife types on her computer in the other room peacefully.
Here, it's dark. I *know*, I just *know*, that if I roll over, face
the even darker spot, I'll see the corpse there, behind me.
And my body shifts uncomfortably the way it does when
you just kind of want to roll over, but I ignore it. Nope.
Not today. It'll be there. I know it.

But, like a child told not to peek, I can't help myself.
I glance behind me. Within the split second, shadows
take on shapes—an arm here, a leg there. No. I turn
my head back, heart pounding. I can still feel the
maggots on my skin, but only on my back, and I know,
I just *know*, that if I glance again, they'll be everywhere,
everywhere, *everywhere*.

In the morning, I almost forget, somehow. I have WiFi
and cellular turned off at first; my laptop is *off* off; I
haven't adjusted the building toy like number blocks
in my little *Wizard of Oz* calendar in my office yet, and I
almost forget, somehow.

I'm tidying, when I come across the notecard I left out
for my wife last night. Among other reminders, I'd added
a dry, *Happy birthday, Farrah.*

Farrah—my schizophrenia tamagotchi, my recurring puppy hallucination—let me know—in the way that imaginary dogs let you know things, like when you realize something in a dream—last year, that July 6th was her birthday. The anniversary. She'd appeared for the first time around the one year anniversary, with the collar whose bright red color hovered *over* it, with the name tag I saw as a mental flash that read *Farrah* for reasons I still haven't figured out. So the timing was about right.

But what do you do for an imaginary dog? I try to telepathically beam her some imaginary biscuits, in the bright white void stored in my brain I imagine she retreats to when she's not out here with me, projected onto the real world.

I whisper it out loud. "Happy birthday, Farrah."

I don't own a lot of memorabilia items at this point. But one of them is the purple dress.

I think it's noble, to keep it, really. I mean, you can't just donate cursed items to Goodwill, or let them run free in a landfill. Some innocent child could find that, *Jumanji* style, you know.

I was wearing the purple dress when I found my father. I was wearing the purple dress when I scrubbed my hands raw next door. I was wearing the purple dress when I scribbled a police report. I was wearing the purple dress when the coroner said, *"You look really young."*

I only wear one thing at a time for various reasons, and at the time, I was wearing that dress, for about a year. It was a simple v-neck, short sleeve, knee length dress. I owned it in many colors. When even the color choice seemed like too much, I cut down to just the green, because it was my wife's favorite, because it brought out my eyes. I wore just the green dress for another year.

During that year, my grandmother died. When the end was coming—weeks after the beginning of a pandemic—I headed over to her house—the one I'd scrubbed my hands raw in, written the police report in—wearing the purple dress, and having packed other colors, because I didn't want the rambunctious dog in the house to ruin one of my current, green dresses.

Grandma was unconscious, had been for a while, and I'd said what needed to be said, made my peace, but I was ready to simply be there, as I told my mom when I was heading there.

Grandma died while I was in the car, driving there from my house a mile away.

I wear something else now. I donated all of those old outfits eventually. Except for the purple dress.

I think I've grieved my father twice, really.

I remember this dream I had in which my best friend died. It was a form of a PTSD dream after my father *did* die, and the striking thing about the dream wasn't the death or the gore—there was none; they died off screen, so to speak. I was worried about them, in the dream; I was at a family party, and many people who are deceased in the real world were with us without question, but I just kept noticing their absence. They were on their way, from work, across town, which they usually commuted to via electric bike. But they were late.

In the dream, I finally thought to check my phone, to look for them on Find My. Even though it wasn't real, I'll always remember the way my stomach sunk when I saw their phone's location was a funeral home. There was an accident. They were gone. It was being processed as evidence.

The dream, after that, was a montage. Days, weeks, months, *years* of unimaginable grief. Talking to their parents. Going through their things. Therapy. Anniversaries. Grieving.

I woke up with a lifetime of trauma I hadn't endured, of grief for someone who had never died.

I did the same thing with my father, in a way; I grieved his death once before he died, in the waking world. In a way, I grieved him when my parents divorced and I went with my mom, too—just his presence.

But, the grieving his death.

It was October 2nd, 2017. I woke up in a dorm in Cambridge I wouldn't live in long and checked my laptop half awake. By the time my eyes opened fully, I was in the hallway, desperately searching for someone who could help me, even though no one could.

The news.

It was everywhere.

Deadliest mass shooting in American history.

Blocks from home. Blocks from *home*, thousands of miles from where I was, pleading for help.

My father wasn't a big *selfie* kind of guy, but he'd sent me one just two days before. *Working this stupid country music festival all weekend,* he'd texted, grinning widely for the camera in a spotlight basket high over the ground. Behind him, Las Vegas Boulevard. Behind him, a window in Mandalay Bay. Most haunted image I've ever seen.

No.

It took hours to get a hold of him. In those hours, I lived a lifetime of grief. I worried for almost everyone I knew, remembering how to breathe every time someone marked themselves safe online, then forgetting again when I realized how many people *hadn't*.

I forgot to breathe sometimes for weeks, until I landed in a psych ward, and then, finally, back home.

Home, where my father had been, fast asleep.

He had, impulsively, taken that night off.

I don't watch TV, really. But not long ago, I got the urge to rewatch *Wall-E.*

I didn't get far. But I thought about the movie a lot.

Dad loved Disney. One of the last texts I ever sent him, one of the few that sat on his phone, undelivered forever, after he wasn't there to see it, before I realized I was texting the void, was that my then girlfriend, now wife, had finally seen *Wall-E.*

She was drunk, after a friend's housewarming party, and to sober her up, a friend and I sat her down in front of the TV we owned back then, with food and Gatorade and *Wall-E*, which is, I must say, still captivating, darkly beautiful. It has no real dialogue for most of the movie, but there is *so much* story, and new things to look at every time you see it. New items grab your attention from the endless landfills Wall-E explores (but there's no cursed purple dress). It's probably good to watch drunk, but I've never been drunk.

Dad loved Disney. He loved Wall-E. The movie, the adorable robot. So I told him that she'd finally seen it, because he considered it a crime otherwise.

He never heard the news, though.

Mom and I talk sometimes about the things we wish we could say to Dad, to Grandma. We've both made our peace with certain things. Do we really need to say *I love you* one more time? No. It's, *I finally found the water shutoff we were always looking for*, or, *She finally watched*

Wall-E, like right after you died. Also, we're married now. By the way.

Today.

Later, my mom takes her car in for a tuneup, and I give her a ride home. We talk about the date. *I lit a candle for your dad.* Happy birthday, Farrah.

We stop before I continue on to my house, and we get out of the car to hug.

And I appreciate every moment we have together, but today, especially, I hug her one second extra long and one squeeze extra tight. I go home and hug my wife one second extra long and one squeeze extra tight.

And, for the people you love, I really hope, today, not tomorrow, you do the same.

TRACKING THE I'LL GIVE YOU SERIES VS. MY MENTAL HEALTH AT THE TIME

I wrote a post a while back: "Tracking Contrivance vs. My Mental Health at the Time," an exercise in tracing changes in my writing versus changes in my mental health.

For this post, I'm doing it again, with the emphasis on the *I'll Give You* series.

(Note: this post was updated to go through the current month, after the original post.)

May 2020

It's been most of a year since the whole "my father died suddenly at fifty-eight and I found his ten day old corpse in his house" thing. I seemed to be over the worst of the trauma response for a little while, but the pandemic struck full force two months ago, reports

about overstuffed refrigerated trucks dominating the
news. My grandmother passed just days ago at home in
hospice care; I arrived just moments after her death to sit
with family.

I've spent most of a year buried in *Contrivance*, my
dark, primary original fiction project of most of a decade,
writing instead of sleeping. My fear of beds—too many
bodies in too many beds, memory and flashback and
nightmare and hallucination—is so bad, I've taken
to sleeping on the floor in the loft (after scaring the
daylights out of my best friend—now our quarantine
roommate in the guest room—by unexpectedly sleeping
on the couch, in the house we closed on the first day of
March). I'm not on meds, and I'm Zooming my therapist
weekly. The world is burning. I just got engaged.

And I need less doom and gloom.

The idea for a new writing project is slowly taking
shape. Daydreams—erotic and otherwise—start to take
real shape, the same characters, situations, themes,
showing up again and again. I could use a distraction,
a little side project. Maybe eighty-thousand words,
I tell myself, a few months, one book. Just a detour
while I figure out a few things about my real writing
love, *Contrivance.* (It's not you, it's me. Maybe we just need
a break.)

I start hashing out character basics, scroll Zillow for
setting inspiration, combining random ideas into a plot.
I sit on the couch and talk it all out with my best friend,
also a writer in need of distraction.

I'm taking an online writing workshop, and our
prompt for a freewrite one day is *company from out
of town could mean trouble.* I misinterpret it slightly
—though the instructor stresses that it's open to

interpretation—and a plot is born, an enemy, a cause, an ending to the story.

I start writing for real, and it's like a dam bursting. I struggle with titles for a bit, but eventually settle on *I'll Give You Everything I Am (You'll Give Me Everything I Want to Be)*. And I start posting it on Archive of Our Own to a silent reception for a full five chapters, because why not?

July 2020

I am still writing like crazy—even winning Camp NaNoWriMo, writing over fifty thousand words in July alone—though I dropped out of the more structured writing workshop. (I finished a shorter one on dialogue, and I notice that this project's dialogue is much more relaxed, natural, than in *Contrivance*, something I want to take with me to my edits.) I'm also picking up a bit of an audience, which is exciting, and a little nervewracking —I've never really written erotica before, not even something centered on romance.

I've also picked up two tricky, additional main characters, whom I battle with—they want to throw grenades at my plot, and I would like them to go away and leave my three-month, eighty-thousand word, one-book side project alone. I retcon them out of past chapters where they're not strictly needed only for them to pop up again, more significantly, later, until we're seriously throwing the word *polyamory* around.

I'm spending a lot of time at the park, on the swingset in triple digit heat, listening to music and trying to figure this project out. Who on Earth are these two, and where do they fit into my beautifully simple, tiny project?

And so Jen and Clara are born.

Meanwhile, my mental health isn't going so well. I'm hallucinating regularly—mostly Dad, dead, and, of all things, a mysterious golden retriever puppy named Farrah. I'm catatonic for hours at a time, occasionally delusional, and generally a mess.

I also start this—*The Schizophrenia Diaries*—because I sure have mental health things to talk about. I'm still maintaining my older blog—more alternative sexuality education—too, and that's now picking up attention from my erotic fiction audience.

My therapist thinks I should go back on meds, but I can't even get in to my old psychiatrist.

Everyone is a mess right now.

August 2020

I've accepted—mostly—that Jen and Clara exist. In Chapter Fourteen, Clara tells Lalia a story that just begs for more, about a time she ran away. In the middle of the night, in the dark, I fire up a new document and title it bluntly "The Night That Clara Ran Away", a title which oddly sticks permanently, and has a few more stories titled in something like parody, like the later "The Night That Clara Just Wanted to Sleep" and "The Night That Evan Ran Away."

So I begin writing companion stories.

September 2020

I'm back on meds, and it's mostly great. I'm sleeping at night, and all but bouncing with energy during the day. I stop seeing my therapist. My best friend moves in with my mom, and I get my own swingset in the backyard.

Vaccines are on the horizon, my wedding is in two months. I've been posting *Contrivance* bits on their own website. A neurologist rules out the idea that I'm having seizures.

In that process, I'm required to do a sleep deprived EEG. So I pull an all nighter. My appointment also happens to be right after Yom Kippur. So I start fasting at sundown, sleep, fast for about twenty-six hours total, eat dinner, and then stay up all night, snacking, and have my morning appointment and then a full afternoon and evening awake, for a total of thirty-eight consecutive waking hours.

If one wasn't psychotic at the start of that, they would be by the end.

And, y'know, I was schizophrenic to start with.

In the middle of the all nighter, I create a Discord server to chat with myself, like a normal person, figuring out *I'll Give You* plot bits. In that crazed night, the plot of what becomes Book Two—by now I've accepted a Book Two is coming—is born.

November 2020

I get married. It is one of the best days of my life, and another one is close on its heels.

I finish what I now acknowledge is only Book One of what I've hesitantly started to call *the I'll Give You series/ trilogy*, and, for fun, have a few copies vanity printed for me and friends. But now that I've put all the formatting work in… why not self publish?

So I do. It's surreal, to hold a published book that arrived in the mail, with hundreds of pages, a real cover, a summary on the back along with reader reviews, a dedication page with my wife's name on it, and my (pen) name on the front.

But… that looks like a book, my mom says when I send her a picture. She had a vague understanding that I was posting erotica online after my best friend blurted it out at dinner, but is surprised—as am I—by the almost four hundred page hardcover in my hands.

Yeah. My quick little side project, indeed.

To my shock, people who aren't my mom even buy it.

December 2020

Encouraged, I start posting *Contrivance* in the same manner—serially, in order, as a book, on Archive of Our Own. It doesn't get quite the same engagement, which is funny to me—*Contrivance* is still my precious baby in a way, not the *I'll Give You* series, but that's okay. Sex sells. I accept that. I'm also accepting I might actually know something about these things I've been writing about, and schedule my first classes as an alternative sexuality educator.

I think I've just about got things figured out—I know how Jen and Clara fit into my no longer so simple plot, I know how I like to post things, I know how self publishing works, I know what has an audience, I know how to talk to my mom about it, I know what's coming in Book Two—and then, Clara tosses another grenade.

She has an eating disorder. Anorexia, specifically. Well, mostly recovered, but it's been there this whole time.

And… it has. It's there, all right—in every time we see her interact with food. It's there, every time she might want a coping mechanism. It's there, in the way she looks in the mirror, in the way she lives in the dance studio, in her penchant for self destruction. It's there, in the former perfectionistic, traumatized teenager without a mother. It's been there.

So I do some research, and I make it work.

February 2021

This whole writing companions thing is kind of out of control, and now there's a book's worth of them, and I publish *The First IGY Companion* as almost an accident.

I've started teaching webinars, I've started going to butler school. Other areas of my life are picking up—not just hunkered down writing.

May 2021

I take a little staycation, a few day writing retreat alone at a nearby hotel, using rewards points that we got to keep through the pandemic.

I don't take care of myself well, though, too lost in my words. My mental state spirals, and I self harm for the first time in many years.

Interestingly, the chapter I'm writing is the one where the main character, Lalia, tries blood play for the first time.

My wife takes me home early, and I recover quickly.

July 2021

By now, I'm running Las Vegas TNG, a local alternative sexuality group, and I publish *Service Slave Secrets (Volume One),* the first years of my blog on the subject, to a nice reception.

Book Two—*I'll Give You Everything I Want to Be (You'll Give Me Everything I Need to Be)*—is flowing, as everyone unpacks their issues in and out of therapy.

I try going off my meds briefly, gradually cutting down with the thought that I'll stop when it starts to affect my sleep, as that's the easiest way to measure the minimum dosage. However, my sleep doesn't really suffer, but I abruptly realize, five minutes overdue for the first dose I've totally skipped, that I've been absolutely miserable, and can't hear my own thoughts over the music hallucinations I mistook for a song stuck in my head, among others.

I go back to the full dosage that night.

November 2021

Several months into the "health kick" that's taken an especially dark spiral recently—hint hint, healthy diets don't include this much purging and fasting and overexercising—I accept that I have an eating disorder—all of the symptoms of anorexia, not quite underweight—and start the cycle of *on again off again* commitment to recovery. I don't need to weight restore, but this cycle has got to stop. I start to talk about it with the people close to me, and write a post in which I theorize about where it came from:

Clara.

It's been almost a year since my abrupt realization that Clara had an eating disorder, and I am now detangling my thoughts and hers. I write a post on this—the dangers of writing a character with a disorder I don't have, as a schizophrenic author with a very fine line between *character* and *self*.

At some point in my research, the tables turned. Now I'm writing backstory companions to pour what *my* head sounds like onto paper—this many calories eaten, this many hours left to fast, this many pounds, BMI this, BMR that, that many minutes of exercise—thoughts that weren't *mine* when I started.

I write about how I took an online eating disorder assessment as research early on, and got a very safe, normal score. Now, though: yup. Something's not right.

Which came first? Was I already developing disordered eating habits, projecting them onto a character until I couldn't deny it was me anymore? I'm convinced that the character's disorder came first, but we'll see.

Incidentally, I finish and publish Book Two instead of winning NaNoWriMo.

March 2022

I publish *The Second IGY Companion* along with *Contrivance* in the same hectic week, having recently finished my first (posted) AU for the *I'll Give You* series: "Let's Not Be Star Crossed Lovers", a short multichapter of alternate backstory.

I'm also finally learning to drive, hallucinations under control, which is always an emotional roller coaster.

Book Three—*I'll Give You Everything I Need to Be (You'll Give Me Everything I Am)*—continues on.

It's certainly an interesting month. I'm still bouncing back and forth on the eating habits, now with my wife's help supervising three meals a day for a while, starting to sort out my disordered thoughts around food, focusing on the fact that skinny seems to represent *productive* for me, and that I'm actually more productive if I just suck it up and eat.

August 2022

Book Three is still in progress, flowing along. A few companions have gone up, but they're slowing down, and I'm thinking of editing them into a future edition of *The Second IGY Companion* rather than creating a third. I have at least one more AU going on in my head to write.

I've gotten into hiking in the last few months, started donating plasma, and started a Little Free Library, and have been working on my newest blog, A Productive Hannah, and am eyeing a brewing sequel to *Contrivance.*

I publish *Service Slave Secrets: Volume Two,* breaking my personal royalty records.

August is a hard month for me, though. I'd like to blame it on hormonal, non psychiatric med changes, but I'm not sure. Right on the heels of some major anniversaries involving my father's birth and death, symptoms, especially the eating issues, flare, and burnout threatens.

I take a week of vacation in Boston, and pledge to take September off from events.

October 2022

I'm back to events, but we've gotten into camping, a welcome reprieve from most of the world. I'm trying to find balance, and overall, my events and writings are going really well. I'm really feeling what's going on in Book Three, and soon to publish *The Schizophrenia Diaries.*

We'll see what the future holds.

THIS IS FOR

This is for the people I shared seventy-two long hours
with
    We'd never met before nor would we ever meet again
    None of us wanted to be trapped within those white,
white walls
    Yet we were all hiding from something out there, too
    This is for them: the crazy, the broken, the silenced
    This is for the roommate I got on my second night,
first full night
    She was blonde, maybe forty, and if we weren't in a
psych ward
    I think she might have been pretty
    But we were
    And she looked like death
    She was detoxing from a drug cocktail from
nightmares
    And neither of us slept
    Since they had to check on us every five minutes
    With lights in our faces all night
    The same drugs that got her here killed her boyfriend
    But she was here to tell me the tale
    And we swapped our stories, and she said,
    "Oh, honey, you don't belong in here,"
    And she told me that I had things waiting for me
outside these white, white walls,

That I should listen to my parents,
And if I wanted to write, then maybe I should write
(And I am)
But no matter what, and I followed this advice, too,
"Don't touch drugs, and don't come back."
This is for the girl with the dark, glossy, staring eyes
That might sound bleak, but she was always smiling, giggling
Her mind was somewhere else, like mine
She was schizophrenic, too,
She'd been there a while,
She told us in a group session that she fell in love with the boy only in her mind
That she believed he would want the best for her, even if it meant his demise
But she just wasn't so sure she wanted to give him up
And I told her I had friends only in my mind, too
And that maybe the ones we really love never truly leave us, real or not real
And medication didn't have to take that away from her
That he'd still be there if she wanted him, but only if she wanted him
But so would the real world now, if she wanted it
And later, I told myself that when I went back on meds,
This thing I said first just to comfort her,
But at that moment, she giggled again, and looked at peace, and said,
"Thank you."
This is for the boy who talked nonstop
He had a sweet, sweet car and a sweet, sweet girl
He couldn't wait to get out and see them both
He told us this over and over and over

And there probably was no car
And there probably was no girl
But God, it was nice to live in his world for a second
He smiled every day over a breakfast a saint couldn't
eat
And didn't mind that you couldn't truly use the
bathrooms alone
He was a regular, knew all the staff's first names
But didn't look over at the sound of his own
And he told us how great the world was out there
And I wanted to believe him
And when they let us walk around the gray courtyard
in circles
For fifteen precious minutes
Instead of hallways paced so much, all night, they put
up signs
Telling you how many laps was a mile
I didn't go outside, because it was pouring
But he went, and he came back in, soaked, radiant
And I asked about the weather, joking, and he told me:
"It's so beautiful."
This is for the one who tried to escape
I saw what he was doing
I cheered him on in my head and looked away,
Don't give him away,
He crouched down low below the nurse's station
And quietly bolted after someone into the locked room
The one with the elevators
But he got caught
And all I could think about was what I would've done
If I'd done it, made it to the first floor
No shoes, no jacket, no wallet, no keys, no phone
They'd taken all of those things away

I would've had only the same clothes I arrived in days
ago
    I wondered if I could've blended in enough to walk out
the hospital's front door
    And then gone... where?
    And I still ask myself that years later,
    And they asked him questions, right then, right there,
    In that white, white hall that told you how many times
you had to pace them
    To get to a mile
    (So many)
    And, bitter, he told them,
    "Well, it was worth a shot."
    This is for someone I don't know
    It was one of us, it could've been any of us
    But I got to borrow one of the hospital's tablets
    To check my school email
    And feel like there was still a world waiting for me
outside
    And right there in the search history
    Was a question we'd all pondered
    Yet I couldn't bring myself to find out the answer
    I didn't want to be a tattle
    But I didn't want to have someone's life on my
conscience
    Even though I'd asked myself the same question
    And I remembered craving death
    The way you're supposed to crave oxygen
    Every second without it throbbing
    I swallowed too many of my antidepressants once
    I regretted it
    I liked to think there really was a worthwhile world
out there

So I told the nurses, just in case
The person I didn't know
Had found the answer to,
"How do you kill yourself in a psych ward?"
This is for the woman who was admitted after me
I overheard them saying she had anger issues, she was delusional
That communication was hard, they said she spoke poor English
She screamed at them that English was her first language,
That they just didn't like that she had dark skin,
That she wasn't born here,
That her accent didn't sound like theirs
She liked to yell and throw and punch
And I was stupid or brave enough to ask her what was wrong once
And she told me she was mad at what the US government had done to her home country in Africa
And I told her that wasn't so delusional, that she was right to be mad
And for what it was worth, I wasn't so fond of what they'd done to this country, either
And she took a deep breath and she told me,
"You seem sane. Don't stop."
This is for the girl who liked to color with me in silence
We weren't supposed to talk about where we came from
But I thought I heard her slip and say something about Harvard
It was around midterm time, then, for both of us
She had scars running up her arms that might scare

the average soldier
    But she made beautiful drawings, with or without lines to color in
    And she doodled hearts over those scars until they faded away
    She just missed her dog, and her mother's cooking,
    And she had a little sister she was scared would turn out just like her
    She didn't say much, but we'd sharpen our pencils under supervision together
    With a cheap little plastic pencil sharpener from a back to school sale
    And I mumbled something about the times I'd taken one of those apart because
    I had nothing else to take out my self hatred with
    In the same breath as complaining about being watched,
    And it was sad, unhinged, shameful,
    But what really made me not want to do it again
    Was when she looked at me with the expression she got
    When she talked about not wanting to scar her sister's wrists
    With her own self loathing, and she said,
    "Same."
    This is for the people I shared only seventy-two long, unwilling hours with
    Complete strangers, yet no matter how different we seemed from each other
    We shared how much the rest of the world wanted to lock us away
    And how much a part of us wasn't quite of that world
    And we did better united than divided

And if I have to be honest
They sure did me a lot more good than the doctors did.

176

MY TYPES OF DISSOCIATION

I've realized that when I talk about dissociating, I can really be talking about a number of different experiences. So I decided to categorize and define some of the versions I talk about most often. This is just my experience, not universal; some aren't even necessarily clinically dissociating at all, but, to me at least, have some kind of resemblance.

Meditative

This one resembles what some people call *productive meditation.* I experience it most often when I go on my morning walk, adding a repetitive, moving element. It's not necessarily bad, and I purposefully invoke it for a reason. But, it's like a form of dissociation to me because it can be very consuming and kind of hard to snap out of. Using the same ritual every morning helps me ease in and out of it at that time, but it can also happen— purposefully or not—at other times. I keep my route very simple, on small streets, and the same every day, *because* I can get pretty lost in my head for this, which is dangerous in other areas. It usually looks like I'm a little lost in thought, though it's more like diving into an internal world entirely. It usually involves decision making, planning, or problem solving, whether it's what I want to work on that day, what my next larger goal should be, or what I should do about (or *if* I should do something about) a problem. Ends more smoothly if I'm done thinking on the topic and have written down any takeaways for later, otherwise I remain very consumed by finishing my loose ends, or keeping track of those takeaways.

Telling a Story

This one kind of feels like productive meditation, except it's less so on purpose. It can also happen during my walks, pretty commonly on the swingset, and at other times. It's not necessarily bad, though it's not very productive, either, and again, consuming and hard to snap out of, though a little less so. This one involves mentally telling a story to a usually ambiguous audience. Sometimes things like blog posts are born of this, but oftentimes it's random anecdotes (or a connected collection of them) from my past, or a recounting of something I've written/media I've consumed. It's kind of like Drunk History, except sober, inside my head, and of personal stories or media. I get very sucked into the story. Often comedic, sometimes touching. If it's a retelling of something I've written (or *sometimes* other media), characters may join in the narration. Sometimes I'll laugh out loud, gesture, and make other matching expressions for this. Ends when the story ends, kind of, though it might loop or expand.

Daydreaming

This is where the story actually happens. This one strikes me pretty much everywhere, on purpose and, frequently, not on purpose, and is probably the most frequent type. Not always bad, though I do write a lot of doom and gloom, angst and tragedy (and even more stays just in my head), and sometimes it's not a great coping mechanism, a form of escapism. This one is especially consuming and hard to snap out of. The real world pretty much goes away entirely, and I at least see and hear (and frequently other senses) as if I'm a fly on the wall in my fictional worlds, or my characters. It often functions much more like a hallucination than a visualization (I also sometimes react in real time as if it is—my eyes track motion or mimic characters' eye movements, so on—or go completely blank); most maladaptive daydreaming descriptions fit, but it still feels like… more. While arguably the most disruptive to my life, I wouldn't give this one up for the world. As a fiction writer, this is where the magic happens.

Thought Loop

When I get kind of stuck in a thought loop of some kind. This could be a general anxious thought, a ritual, or an eating disorder thought train. I really noticed this the other day while my wife and I were getting ready to leave the house. I realized that in the external world I was standing there, still, silent, staring blankly at nothing, long enough my wife was like, "… 'Kay. I'll go cool the car down." It frequently looks like this, or you might see mumbling/counting on fingers, or actually doing the actions, sometimes anxiously or repetitively.

What was going on in my head, however, was mentally running through my *leaving the house* rituals. I have many rituals like this, for everything from leaving the house to cleaning the kitchen, and they have a hard time changing. I later explained to my wife that one bullet point I had in my head, for leaving the house, was the word *dogs*, which meant that I should give the dogs their treats before I leave. We don't have dogs. This bullet point comes from when my mom and I lived on our own in a rental house briefly after my parents' divorce, and I would give our two dogs some treats before I went on a walk to the park… eight years ago. At least one of those dogs is dead now, and probably both. Still, my mental rituals change on *years* of delay, with a lot of conscious work if I really feel the need to put it in, so, in that moment, I had to check *gave the dogs their treats* off in my head (several times, as I frequently go through all of my related rituals until I've reached something not checked off, do that thing, and then start over, then go through them like twice after everything has been checked off). This can be brief, but completely consuming, and I get much more anxious if I am pulled away from in it any way. In a way, I can't function without this, but due to the rituals not being malleable, and how many times I have to go through them, it's mostly unproductive. I'm currently trying to focus on having the important parts written down, and looking at those lists a reasonable amount, not going through old rituals in my head over and over.

Blank/Zoned Out

The one where nothing's going on in my head. You

see the blank stare, and that's actually all there is. I don't get it a lot, and this tends to be a stress response, so it's almost nice when it does happen, a reset to neutral, though it's ultimately escapism. I might also just be that tired. Everything goes away. I could live without it, and it's not the most common, though it's often what people assume is going on when I get the blank stare. Completely consuming and hard to snap out of. Hard to do on purpose, and I generally don't. Frequently goes with being nonverbal (or at least serious flat affect/monosyllabic responses) and/or catatonic. Frequently ends in sleep.

Sensory Overload

Occurs when I'm in sensory overload. Not much is going on in my head typically—distracted attempts at escapism or coping, generally, or really, really trying to focus. I might look jumpy and distracted, frustrated, or somewhat catatonic (or be actually trying to escape the onslaught, closing my eyes, covering my ears, etc.). Could definitely live without this one. Less so *consuming* and moreso *distracting,* can't really engage when I'm in it. Frequently renders me nonverbal. Never on purpose. Breaks only when I escape whatever's causing the sensory issue for a while, usually after a bit of lag.

Active Delusion

Occurs when I am in the grips of a new/active delusion. Somewhat rare with meds and all. Most common subtype might be more of a depersonalization—like looking in the mirror, sometimes literally, often not, and thinking, *Is that really me?* The only thing in my mind is usually thinking through the delusion—sometimes leaning away from it, trying to logic myself out of it, other times, building it up, defending it, finding out what it *is.* I tend to be talking about it, very quickly, or possibly catatonic/nonverbal. Mostly not in touch with reality. Could definitely live without this one, too. Never done on purpose. Completely consuming, very hard to snap out of. Solved mostly by time and sleep. Delusions have been about anything from believing in the existence of magical notebooks to believing neither my wife nor my usual pharmacy existed.

Depression Urges

Rare, kind of. Occurs in phases. Happens when I feel extremely depressed, usually in a more anxious way. Looks like: desperately trying to self harm, or else very twitchy if I'm trying to resist, possibly trying to distract myself. Might do anything from laugh to seem frustrated. On the inside, there's the obsession, usually racing and anxious thoughts, existential, that sound like depression. (The psychologist who gave me my diagnoses had a theory that I never had depression at all, only anxiety, and I see where she's coming from when I examine what these thoughts look like.) Yeah, could live without this one, but it's also weird to think about my personality without it, or without where it comes from, at least. Not done on purpose, though it might look like it; I'm not really *me* when it's full blown. Consuming, hard to come out of on purpose, but I tend to snap out of it abruptly and within a few hours at most. If I do succeed in self harming, it stops, though it usually turns into something like Blank/Zoned Out.

Hallucination/Flashback/Waking From Nightmare

When I am partially consumed by something that isn't real. This type varies wildly, really, but I couldn't think of any further ways to break it down. Happens in phases, overall somewhat frequent. Not done on purpose. Might look anxious/scared (sometimes visibly shaking), distracted, twitchy/jumpy, staring at a certain spot, overall reacting to seemingly nothing, or suddenly zone out briefly and repeatedly. Could largely live without this one. I'd keep the dog, I guess. Partially to totally consuming, sometimes responds well to distraction, or will fade with sleep/time. I might be going somewhere else entirely (the dog's/Farrah's white void she hangs out in, the whole scene of my trauma, back into the nightmare) or seeing something projected onto the real world (corpse, dog, etc.) Could also involve other senses, especially auditory (voices, music, etc.) and tactile. Sometimes terrifying, sometimes amusing, sometimes just distracting or unnerving. I have another post in mind about most common hallucinations...

MY MOST COMMON HALLUCINATIONS

A very common first question when talking about psychosis is, "What do you hallucinate?" It's not an incredibly simple question; it's kind of like asking someone, "What do you see, in general?" Of course, it varies person to person, but here are my most frequent hallucinations, in no particular order.

Voices, Chatter, Noise

Voices saying specific things, or general chatter around me. The latter version is more common for me, and when I say I hear voices, the next question is always *what do they say.* But it's kind of like if you're sitting in a crowded restaurant, and someone asks you, "What are people talking about?" I'm not necessarily paying attention. There are some words I can't make out at all. Often there are random noises in the mix. Some voices I might recognize repeatedly, whether or not I can make out what they're saying. Some things I can *barely* understand. Random phrases I catch, meaningless, completely out of context. I might be able to tune in to one voice or exchange at a time. (I also sometimes, less frequently, get the random noise without any chatter/voice element.)

Other times, I do hear only one or two voices saying more specific things. People talking about me, at times like when I'm in an empty public bathroom (usually not nicely). An echo of something random I heard or read, or a conversation I had earlier, often repeatedly. Brief back and forths with imaginary versions of people I know, often unpleasant. Someone calling my name (a rather common experience for many people). My characters talking, more to each other than me, isolated from the rest of their world. (My characters more frequently appear to me in other ways that resemble hallucinations, which I discussed more in the types of dissociation post and elsewhere). Or, my thoughts kind of splitting off into a second voice, until I realize I'm not controlling the second voice anymore. So on.

Lights/Blobs

Flickering lights, fireworks, flames, flashes of lightning, cloudlike blobs, often indoors, all colors. Sometimes pretty and easily blocked out, sometimes distracting and encroaching on the center of my vision, especially the ominous dark blobs that sometimes come before the flashback hallucinations.

Music

Music, in general. Especially when I've recently listened to the same song on repeat or to a lot of music that sounds similar—my brain will play it, often gradually louder and louder, in a much more real way than having a song stuck in my head, until

I next fall asleep and wake up with it faded or gone.
(I can also, at other times, kind of do this at will, like
it's a real radio in the background while I do other
things.) Certain artists seem to trip it more than others,
which sometimes informs my listening choices, and
it's often not ones you'd think of as catchy. (My brain
really likes Evanescence, for starters.) I've also had a
phase for playlists of, say, piano music, lead to days of
hallucinations of piano music, no song in particular,
just… piano. I've had the same happen with ASMR files,
though those usually mimic one file in particular. Same
for movie soundtracks; my brain just kind of invents
music that sounds like it *could've* been from that movie,
but wasn't. I threw a *Harry Potter* themed party earlier
this year and had all the scores playing for several
hours… and remixes for several hours more only in my
head (louder and louder until I fell asleep). Same for
the *Star Wars* party.

Notifications

Any sound that functions as a notification. Our
doorbell, my alarm clock sound, my wife's alarm clock
sound, any familiar ringtone, so on. I'll hear it once
at random (this is also fairly common), or every few
minutes for a few hours or so, or I'll hear it on constant
repeat, sometimes for days at a time. Usually starts
sometime shortly after I actually heard the sound.
Definitely reduces the effectiveness of my actual alarms,
so I mix up the sound now and then.

Flashbacks

Hallucinations related to my PTSD, that go beyond the typical flashbacks. Typically the corpse—sometimes this is a distortion of a living person I am actually seeing —sometimes the death smell, and frequently the feeling of maggots, even though I didn't experience it myself. Easily triggered by seeing anything similar (including in television, certain Halloween decorations, etc.), people staying very still/sleeping (especially unexpectedly), beds (especially white linens, which I mostly don't use), darkness/shadows/certain black things, and anniversaries related to deaths in the family/those people when they were alive.

Farrah, Farrah's Void

I've talked about Farrah a lot here, but: a golden retriever puppy who appears to me regularly via assorted visual, auditory, and tactile hallucinations that sometimes match up more than others, who seems to represent the part of my brain that wants to be psychotic and creative. She kind of glows and hovers and makes faces that real dogs don't make, teleports at times, and I'm kind of telepathic with her; it's like she can think things at me that manifest as kind of auditory hallucinations, and kind of the way you suddenly understand information in dreams. She started appearing around the one year anniversary of my father's death and has been in and out since. She came with a collar and a name tag; I didn't choose the name. She's very reactive to the real environment, but sometimes is in her Void: an endless white abyss in my brain I sometimes visit by varying levels of accident if I dissociate hard enough. I call her my schizophrenia tamagotchi. Sometimes I wish she'd come out and play even more.

Distortions

Distortions of real objects. Flickering, changing colors, sizes, orientation, details, and being off of where they actually are. Think Alice in Wonderland, or the types of hallucinations associated with certain drugs. I gave one specific example under *flashbacks.* Very, very bad to have while driving, and I already have spatial reasoning issues. Sometimes just makes me look even more clumsy, closing my fingers around the empty space *next* to something. Especially hard to explain or catch as a hallucination sometimes, since we'll both see the object itself in some way.

SCHIZOPHRENIA IN CREATIVITY AND PRODUCTIVITY

(Note: This post has been adapted for The Schizophrenia Diaries, but is mostly a repost from A Productive Hannah.)

In some ways, I honestly don't remember much around the origins of this blog. It was summer 2020 (and let's face it—who has a great memory of summer 2020?). I wasn't yet back on antipsychotics (by weeks to months), I was facing a pandemic, a world on fire, the recent death of my grandmother, and the one year anniversary of discovering my father's death (leading to PTSD). I was mostly lost in a creative haze, spending hours every day on the swingset at the nearest park in heat over 110*F—dissociatively daydreaming up new plotlines with a song on repeat—or curled up in the fetal position on the floor in my office, near catatonic and hallucinating. It was A Time.

However, it was one of the most prolific periods of my life. After spending most of a year after my father's death pouring emotions into *Contrivance*, my primary fiction project of almost a decade, instead of sleeping at night, I was (mostly) taking a break from *Contrivance's* dystopian doom and gloom that now seemed all too realistic, focusing on what I thought would be a quick, simple side project to perk me up, which eventually became the *I'll Give You* series, my first real foray into erotica, which now has four books published and more in the works (spoiler alert: not a quick, simple, or always cheery side project after all).

And, I started The Schizophrenia Diaries, after having casually maintained a different blog for about a year. My first post wasn't about writing or creativity at all. It was about Farrah, my so called schizophrenia tamagotchi, my recurring puppy hallucination, who had recently come about. From there, I wrote about all manner of mental health related things for about six months, essays as ideas came up, then floundered a little on what to do with the blog. I was back on meds, and out of therapy. Vaccines were on the horizon. The election was over. I'd recently gotten married and published my first book. Things were good, and while I was grateful, I wasn't sure what to write about now; without acute symptoms to reflect on, I got a little lost. Things on the blog slowed down, and I didn't make a post in 2021 until mid April.

I had thought about it in the meantime. I didn't really want to abandon the blog. Schizophrenia is highly stigmatized and misunderstood. Stories of schizophrenics are rarely told at all, and even more rarely do we get to tell our stories ourselves. I felt it was important—part of something bigger than me—to write on it. But, the blog was neglected when I was doing well, which gave me mixed feelings on it, and I wasn't sure what I had left to say. I thought that maybe I needed more of a theme, an angle, something to ground the project besides processing symptoms as they arose.

I reread some early posts on the blog. What grabbed me was my last post before things really slowed down, a September post before two more that December and then silence for four months. (Note: I know I made some posts that were later taken down, so there may be minor inaccuracies here.) The post that grabbed my attention was about psychosis as a part of my writing process, how my schizophrenia and my colloquial tortured artist syndrome intertwined, about how my psychotic daydreams fueled my writing, how the darkness of the things I tended to write about both contradicted my triggers and calmed me down, and so on.

That. That was my angle. Because even when my symptoms *improved*, they were still there—and the most cohesive way I could talk about them was through how they impacted my creative processes. No matter what, I was always writing. I always had that to talk about.

With reframing and revising, things picked up on the blog again, even when my mental health was largely okay.

I talk a lot about psychosis and creativity—but what about psychosis and *productivity*, one of my other passions?

I mentioned that one of the worst time periods in my life as far as symptoms was also one of my most prolific— how does that work?

There's definitely a balance.

After having made it without meds for about two years, when I started again, the first night I took Seroquel —well, firstly, it knocked me out so unexpectedly hard and fast that I fell out of my chair at my desk—the change was immediate. For a few days, I was basically symptom free. It was almost like I didn't have schizophrenia, overnight. I realized how bad my sleep had been—which didn't help anything. It had been so bad, I realized, as Seroquel knocked me out at night, I wondered if I could chalk almost everything that year up to sleep deprivation, the miracle of Seroquel to the miracle of sleep, more than its use as an antipsychotic.

But during those few days, I felt… conflicted.

When Farrah—the dog who's not real, mind you—found out—when *I* decided—that I was likely going back on meds, she worked those puppy dog eyes real hard. *Why would you want to get rid of me, Mom?* I tried to telepathically communicate to her that as far as I was concerned, I was happy to keep her, if I could get rid of the corpse and the blaring music and the black blobs and the flashes of light and the white noise and the maggots and all of the other issues. Later, I came to realize that Farrah—this is my current working theory, at least—represents the part of my mind that *wants* to be psychotic, freely creative without the limits of pesky reality.

During those first few days after Seroquel, I felt… a little empty. Numbed. Better than I had in months, maybe a year, in certain ways, but… something was missing. My daydreams were missing, my fiction fuel— they were back in the normal human range. It was like watching a movie on a decades old television versus watching it in IMAX 3D. I couldn't get reality to go away entirely even when I tried—and normally, I didn't have to try; in fact, normally, I had to fight to get back when my alarm went off telling me it was time to make dinner or something, nudging me out of daydreams.

Despite how well I seemed to be doing, I wondered if I

might lower the dosage.

But, my body quickly adjusted. A few days later, I *could* sink into my daydreams that deeply again, but I had some more control over starting, and I didn't have to fight quite as hard to stop. Other symptoms stayed *improved* but didn't vanish. And, not lost in the daydream stage forever, it was easier to get out when I wanted, to grab a pen, and start putting daydreams on paper. But things can get pretty bad—lots and lots of time lost in fantasy on the verge of hallucination, not quite in my control—before I totally stop getting to the part where I write them down. After meds, I was overall *less* purely prolific, except for a few really, really bad parts of that prior year or so.

However, that was just about fiction word count. I thrived in other areas like I never had before, where psychosis was mostly a burden. It's not much of an advantage as far as being a housewife, a landlord, a butler school student, an alternative sexuality educator, a group organizer, or even a nonfiction writer (overall, my *blogging* writing has picked up since). In fact, those last three non writing areas were all things I seriously picked up within a year *after* meds for the first time. I found more balance. I wrote a little less fiction at times (we're still talking frequently upwards of 25,000 words per month), but I did everything else that was productive a little more, more than enough to fill the gap.

Even my fiction did pick up a more *productive* edge, though. Things other than sheer word count matter for that. Pieces actually got finished, typed, edited, formatted, and posted, in a largely linear way that didn't contradict itself, with improved quality. More than the three people closest to me began to read it.

I see this *psychosis equals creativity but lack of balance* thing in my past, too. My schizophrenia was early onset. My symptoms first appeared around my fifteenth birthday, mid ninth grade. I was producing writing like crazy—even winning multiple rounds of National Novel Writing Month per year (this means writing upwards of 50,000 words in a month—many times, I got closer to 100k). However, school wasn't going so well. I dropped out before the end of tenth grade. Now, I see why I was writing fiction like crazy while failing to turn in five-hundred word essays that weren't word salad gibberish, or be non catatonic long enough to show up to class, or finish taking a test without yelling at demons only I could see.

So are there pros to schizophrenia for productivity, for me, as a fiction author? Yes. In other areas? Less so that I see right now, though I frequently joke that my general, various anxious neuroses are the edge that keeps me moving so quickly, lest I die tomorrow. Are there cons? Of course. Many. Still, I wouldn't quite hit the *cure* button, for myself.

It's just, as many other things are, about balance.

WHY WE NEED DIVERSE STORIES (A LETTER I WROTE IN A DREAM)

When I was in high school, I started writing my own happy endings.

I was fifteen, in love with another girl, drowning in homework, developing schizophrenia, and generally more confused than ever.

Then came yet another English project, which included doing research on a chosen subject and then writing about it in ten different genres/formats. A Multi Genre Research Portfolio of Fun, if you will. Or, the MGRPOF. There were multiple all nighters and trips to craft stores involved in this Portfolio of Fun for most of us, and it was due immediately after an annual, weekend long field trip for my major that was basically a sacred tradition, making many of us in the program, including me, miss it.

Still. Not yet out, I dared to push the envelope a little and selected my topic: mental health and LGBTQ+ young adults.

I researched. I discovered the Butterfly Project, years before I needed it. I read *Raising My Rainbow* by Lori Duron (and keep up on that family to this day). I read countless articles.

For one of my genres, I selected the short story, but instead of the one or two pages required, I ended up writing sixty, and split it into sections. Each section ended in a piece that fit into that same story—though the project didn't have to all go together—in another format option offered: a love letter, a diary entry, a speech, a poem, a news article.

And through this portfolio, I created a future I could see myself fitting into. Here are two young women in college, one struggling with depression and being openly queer despite her dubious and religious upbringing, the other closeted and questioning, too anxious to commit and come out, still thinking of the straight girl in high school who got away. Here is how they fall in love: the close friendship typical among young women that goes further and further. Here is them dancing together when their male dates vanish, here is them taking on stigma hand in hand, here is the kiss they share at a pride rally when everything feels okay.

Here is a world for me beyond a husband, two point five kids, and a dog.

My final submission was all arranged together in a scrapbook. I still have that scrapbook. It is not an archive of my past, but an archive of the first future I saw for myself filled with that kind of love, after I started having so many questions.

And now...

I don't have a husband, or two point five kids, or a dog. (Well, there's always the imaginary one.) I have a wife, and two cats (and I'm petitioning for number three), and a house on the end of a cul de sac with a metaphorical white picket fence, and a white SUV, and a conglomeration of things I do, that I love, and that aren't such shocking choices; yet there was a time I couldn't see this future coming.

And still, sometimes, I seek out my past. I seek it out in the young adult section of the library that is, both slowly and all at once, catching up.

Here are stories about hopeless crushes on queer Internet friends that you've never gotten to meet, but rush home to talk to, text under the table in class. Here are stories with teenagers running to therapy appointments after school, doing homework in waiting rooms, or running to synagogue, doing public school homework under the table with Hebrew papers on top, and asking the Rabbi the hard questions; *is it okay to be gay? What if you don't believe?* Here are stories with girls falling asleep on each other on the bus, holding hands while they walk home from the bus stop and wondering if it means what they think it means. Here are stories with *practice kissing* and stolen glances at your best friend while doing homework together. Here are stories about Googling words you discovered in fan fiction erotica, that sound a whole lot like you.

Here are stories that make me feel like any of it ever made any sense, enough sense that maybe someone else could've gone through it, too. Here are the stories I put in my *read in color* Little Free Library, so that everyone else can read them, too.

Here are the stories I write, for the people who need them most. Readers tell me over and over how they cling to my characters that resemble them, because they're not cis or straight or vanilla or monogamous or abled or neurotypical or White or Christian or male. How it feels to be seen, to see themselves, past, present, and future, to be represented.

And that's why we need diverse stories.

But sometimes even I wonder if we still need them. Are there enough now? Look at the Internet. Look at the world. We've come so far. So many things are more visible. Yet we've slipped back so much, too. And are stories worthy? Or should all that time go to other activism?

But then my mind provides me a memory: sitting at a pancake brunch with an elderly family member, glowing, radiant, as she tells me she is so glad to have lived into her eighties to finally get to watch a few characters who are like her on primetime television.

And then I stop asking silly questions, pick up my pen, and get back to work.